faith
and
virtue

faith and virtue

by DAVID BAILY HARNED

A PILGRIM PRESS BOOK
from United Church Press
Philadelphia, Pennsylvania

Library of Congress Cataloging in Publication Data

Harned, David Baily.
  Faith and virtue.
  "A Pilgrim Press book."
  Includes bibliographical references.
  1. Virtue. 2. Virtues. 3. Christian ethics.
I. Title.
BV4630.H37   241'.4   73-5686
ISBN 0-8298-0250-9

The scripture quotations are, unless otherwise indicated,
from the *Revised Standard Version of the Bible,* copyright 1946 and 1952 by the Division of Christian Education, National Council of Churches, and are used by
permission.

The quotations from *The Four Cardinal Virtues* by Josef
Pieper are copyright © 1965 by Harcourt Brace Jovanovich, Inc. and are reprinted by their permission.

The material from *The Spire* by William Golding is
copyright © 1964 by William Golding and is reprinted by
permission of Harcourt Brace Jovanovich, Inc.

The excerpt from *Death of a Salesman* by Arthur Miller
is copyright 1949 by Arthur Miller. All rights reserved.
Reprinted by permission of The Viking Press, Inc.

United Church Press, 1505 Race Street, Philadelphia, Pennsylvania 19102

contents

preface

Faith and Virtue was written in three places that hold particular significance for me. A preliminary sketch was finished while I was professor of Christianity at Punjabi University, Patiala, India, during 1970–71. I am grateful to the National Endowment for the Humanities for the award of a fellowship that enabled me to revisit Patiala with my family during the first semester of that year. Then a draft of the entire manuscript was written during the months we had at our summer home in Northfield, Massachusetts, during 1971 and 1972. The final version was completed during the first semester of 1972–73, while I was visiting professor in the department of Christian dogmatics at the University of Edinburgh. Several chapters of the book were first delivered as lectures there. I want to record my gratitude for the award of a Sesquicentennial Associateship by the Center for Advanced Study at the University of Virginia, which enabled me to be in Scotland again with my family. My host during those months, Prof. Thomas F. Torrance, was my first teacher of theology and he remains very much my teacher still.

Books are partnerships in many ways: between author and reader, a man and his colleagues, a teacher and his students, a student and some teachers now retired or gone. I am indebted to a number of friends who read these pages in one form or another, and from whose criticisms and suggestions I have gained much profit. As well as Professor Torrance, at Edinburgh Dr. Robin Gill of the department of Christian ethics has offered valuable advice. At the University of Virginia, there is Prof. James F. Childress: he has read everything that I have written during the last five years, and from his generous encouragement and careful criticism I have received more than anyone has a right to hope to gain from a colleague. I also want to mention Dr. Julian N. Hartt, who is Kenan Professor of Religious Studies at Virginia, and Kevin F. Dale, who as a student has never failed to teach those who taught him. I owe a very special debt to Prof. Stanley Hauerwas of the department of theology at the University of Notre Dame. He has read the essay with great care and offered many suggestions; it is far better than it could have been without his assistance. No one has taught me as much about theological ethics in a very long time.

This essay is dedicated to my sons, Christopher and Timothy, in the hope that someday they will know more about these things than their father has learned and perhaps as much as their mother does.

David Baily Harned

Advent, 1972
Edinburgh

introduction

Faith and Virtue is a sequel to Grace and Common Life, sharing with it a concern for the importance of vision and imagination in human conduct. Another essay is intended to deal with the ear and with the significance of listening, and together they are offered as part of a sketch of a modest brand of natural theology. That discipline has come upon hard times, and for many people, not least of all for many theologians, it has all the promise and contemporary relevance of alchemy. Perhaps its situation can be remedied, however, if it is treated as though it were an unhealthy shrub and transplanted, shifted from a place where it will not grow and rooted in different soil. I, too, am skeptical of it as an independent discipline, but I am equally convinced of its value as a moment within a confession of faith. By natural theology, I mean a discipline that accepts the truth of revelation in Jesus Christ and then examines the texture of our ordinary experience for its witness to the holy, without any pretense of immaculate neutrality. In its role as servant of theological confession, it has many services to provide.[1]

When one explores the multifoliate varieties of faith that sustain men and the households of gods that faith sustains as the final sources of whatever meaning and value existence holds, it is apparent that our humanness is most threatened not by "atheism and materialism" but by our spiritualizing of life and consequent godriddenness. One of the uses of natural theology is to disclose where wraiths of old gods still reign and where flabby new ones exercise their emergent hegemonies. Even if such exposure will not exorcize all the divinities that harass us, at least it can arm us better against them and preclude too simple or too rapid resolution of questions that concern where men ought ultimately to place their bets.

Second, the surfaces of our experience are scored by all sorts of rifts and faults and crevasses. It is a mystery that they should be there, and they intimate greater mysteries within themselves. If natural theology cannot prove the existence of God, at least by beginning with God it need not end without him. It can focus our attention on the many and various ways that the world points beyond itself, on all the instances of transcendence that abound in our common life and that suggest instances greater still, on thirsts within the self too imperious to be easily denied and ordered toward more than the factual realm can ever provide. If the enterprise can yield no answers, it does more than enough to keep the questions alive.

Third, by continuing to speak of natural theology we can stress the obdurate thereness and integrity of the ingredients of this world. We can acknowledge the need to take them seriously for what they are in and of themselves, and thereby recall our own selves from what sometimes seems to be an incorrigibly manipulative stance toward reality. One sort of secularization in the modern world that is really inimical to traditional piety lies in the assumption that we can equate the whole of reality with what we can manipulate. Natural theology can offer its own contribution to moral reflection because the greatest problem of vision and especially of the virtue of prudence, on which the welfare of every other virtue hangs, is simply to pierce the veil of our selfishness and to recognize that something else is real, really other than ourselves and resisting our manipulative touch.

Finally, and most important of all, natural theology can anchor confessional statements in the texture and density of our common life and provide some remedy for the gnosticism that perennially afflicts Christian thought, clarifying the significance of faith for the illumination of small joys and confusions and hardships, refusing to allow language about God to lose touch with the immediacies and ambiguities of our condition. To whatever extent it succeeds in weaving the stuff of our ordinary experience together with the words of ancient creeds, the unity will bring new luster and richness to the pleasures and cares of the everyday world. Some writers will quarrel with the continued use of the phrase "natural theology," of course. But if this usage is controversial, it seems no more controversial than the conclusions of natural theology have usually been when the discipline was more traditionally conceived. Perhaps it will flourish in soil cultivated by faith, and perhaps the transplanting of it to acknowledge its Christian commitment does nothing more than render explicit what has too often been covertly presupposed. After all, it is doubtful whether natural theology has ever functioned significantly except for those already persuaded by faith.

Faith and Virtue does not address these concerns as directly as its predecessor did, but they are reflected especially in the insistence upon the dialectical character of healthy faiths, hopes, and loves. This is the subject of chapters 3 and 4. In the loss of the essential dialectic we can trace the provenance of the *daimon* gods that haunt the human commonwealth; in its loss, too, we are confronted by religious pretensions that arise endlessly within the city of man and that endure because they prey upon the irrepressible hopes and desires written into creatures who are destined always to crave more than the factual order can muster. Again, the stress upon the importance of faith, hope, and love for every version of common life is intended to display both the congruence and the conflict between Christian faith and natural community as well as the cruciality of basic trust for all life together. The pervasiveness as well as the ordinarily flawed nature of these virtues renders Christian claims intelligible and interesting.

Then, too, the interpretation of the church as an instance of speaking with strangers is intended to serve the argument that the "natural" virtues, because of their dependence upon prudence, are crippled and inhibited by our universal xenophobia, unless we find reasons that constrain us to seek out the stranger and to hear the crucial lessons that he must teach us all. Perhaps most important is the argument that vision rather than principle is the real determinant of conduct, that vision depends upon images, that the image most appropriate for the governance of moral life is the image of the self as player, and that this is a fair expression of the anthropological implications of the disclosure of God. Our principles are derived from the stories we have heard. The stories and their imagery tell us of the faiths of other men, kindle faith in us, provide us with perspectives. Every perspective involves a sort of faith; the question is not whether we will have faith but what faith we will have. These contentions are discussed especially in chapters 2 and 8.

The idea of the holy and the notion of virtue are legacies from lands separated by the waters of the Mediterranean; they involve different and sometimes antagonistic assumptions. In the first of their two greatest encounters, Augustine characterized pagan virtue as nothing more than splendid vice. In the second, of course, Thomas made the language of virtue an integral part of the Christian tradition. But there is good reason for Christian skepticism of the idea, and classical Protestantism objected to this aspect of the Thomistic synthesis no less than to many of its other elements. One objection is that the vocabulary has often been used to argue that our fundamental problem concerns the relationship of reason and appetite: human excellence emerges as man manages to conform his animal nature to the dictates of rationality. The biblical tradition is far more suspicious of reason, however, and locates the source of man's fallenness not in what he shares with other animals but in what is most distinctively his own, not in carnality but in spirit. In other words, at least from one Christian perspective, the idea of virtue simply mislocates the problem. But this is a deficiency that is not necessarily inherent in the language of virtue. If we recognize the existential disruption of the dialectical structure of faith, hope, and love, as well as the way that certain forms of these virtues, flawed though they may be, are presupposed in the cultivation of all others, it is certainly possible to find the cause of man's fallenness in his highest and most distinctively human ambitions. This argument occupies much of chapter 4.

The idea of virtue tells of something that man achieves for himself and possesses as his own immanent resource against the outrages of fortune. Sometimes it has seemed difficult to reconcile this perspective with the biblical insistence that man's recovery of his relationship with God depends wholly upon a *justitia aliena* that is lost in the moment that an individual grasps to make it his own. A consistent refrain of this essay, though, is that a satisfactory interpretation of the virtues says nothing more eloquently than that there is little we have that we have not received from others. But the achievement of virtue depends upon the condition of our vision no less than it does upon gifts from other selves. As I shall so frequently reiterate, we are free for choice and deliberate action only within the world that we can see, and it is not easy to see. Because vision is shaped by whole galaxies of images of the world and of the self, the exploration of virtue quickly brings us within the precincts of the imagination. The biblical tradition says little about imagination, however; it insists that the avenue by which the holy addresses man is not the eye but the ear. Still, the reference to a particular sense is a metaphorical description of a certain form of human response and by no means a rejection of the importance of sight.

Finally, virtues have often been described as "rational habits" and "operative skills." Although there are some forms of love and justice that fit this description, there is little sense in applying such language to faith in God or love for him. But the root of the problem is that this language suggests a particular interpretation of the nature of the self. The idea of virtue has become rather disreputable because it has been associated with an understanding of selfhood that has been severely criticized. I have avoided a technical vocabulary because I do not want to opt for a certain model of man and I do not believe that the notion of virtue demands one particular option. So it has been of great importance to maintain a certain vagueness in references to intentions and motives, appetites and agency and disposition. The elaboration of a particular moral psychology is beyond the scope of this essay, and all the more so because it suggests that the significance of the idea of virtue is restricted to a certain model of selfhood when it is, or so I believe, relevant to every consideration of what humanness means.

Grace and Common Life charted some intimations of grace in ordinary experience, tracing times when the self is surprised by gifts that it could neither expect nor deserve. These occasions call men to reflect more carefully upon the anatomy of their experience and suggest, at least to the eyes of faith, the presence and activity of a power that transcends the world. The essay explored the dimensions that grace always possesses, no matter whether human or divine—community, acceptance, the sort of enrichment of imagination that expands the powers of the self, and the opportunity for creativeness—and argued that when persons acknowledge themselves to be in the presence of the holy they can best understand their new situation in terms of images drawn from the family and from play. Nothing is ultimately serious except for what alone is ultimate, the reality of God; therefore, the anthropological implications of the Christian story can be distilled in the master image of the self as player. By this image of himself man can best grasp the dialectic of his freedom from a world that is less than God, and his obligation to abide always by rules of fairness, because he too is less than God and is no more than one among many creatures who are all involved in the same game.

This companion essay is partly an examination of some of the gifts that accrue to the self when it acknowledges that it lives before God—and especially of the "theological" virtues of faith, hope, and love, which have long been described within the Christian tradition as "effects of grace." The connection between the essays does not rest only upon conventional linguistic usage. The counsel of the "natural" virtues of temperance and justice and courage is that men should play fair; the study of virtue, then, brings flesh and sinew to an image of man as player that is initially skeletal, enabling us to discriminate among various forms of playing, some of which are consonant with faith in God, some of which are not. On the other hand, the dictates of the "natural" virtues find their most profound justification and support in the image of the self that is implied by the disclosure of the holy. Furthermore, because human action is inconceivable apart from stories and from images of the self as agent, in the principle of fairness that is expressed by the contents of temperance, justice, and courage there is at least an adumbration of or a yearning for the figure of man as player and the interpretation of life as a game. In both essays, therefore, the idea of fair play and the master image of man as player are crucial, although there is no explicit attention to the definition of fairness or to the clarification of what is intended by the use of "master image" until chapter 8.

The generally theological and specifically Christian perspective of these pages is reflected in the insistence that the idea of virtue cannot be explored satisfactorily without extensive reference to the Christian community. No lacuna in earlier treatments of the same theme is so obvious or damaging. The reason for attention to the church has nothing to do with a desire to restrict to Christians alone the title to virtue. But virtues are born from our social experience, and what we can do depends upon what has first been done to us and for us by other selves; so it would be puzzling indeed to refer to Christian virtue without reference to a Christian context. No variety of faith or hope can long sustain itself without some "plausibility structure,"[2] as though it made no difference whether or not we were isolated from conversations with significant others who share the same faith and reaffirm a common hope. It is necessary to examine the consequences of membership in various plausibility structures and the variety of ways that they either engender or inhibit the attainment of virtue. Still, the attention to the relationship between virtue and religious community in this essay has a different rationale.

The vocation of the Christian community is best understood in dialectical terms. On the one hand, the church is a mediator, invested with certain priestly roles, awarded various interpretive functions, entrusted with a word to proclaim; on the other, it is an instance of speaking with strangers, speaking with them simply because they can always be found somewhere outside the door. This interpretation of the task of the church is not meant to describe merely an ancillary and subordinate function but reaches to the core of its nature, for only in this way can the community proclaim its own origin and essence as a band of those who were befriended while they were yet strangers, enemies and ungodly. Nor does the church know any God except him who comes in the guise of the stranger. There is an important conjunction of this aspect of the life of the community and the notion of virtue, because prudence means that we are liberated from the vise of our selfish preoccupations so that we no longer block our own vision but can grasp the strangeness, the otherness and apartness of the realm of the actual. There is no better tutelage in prudence than what is afforded by the encounter with the stranger, but we are wary of strangers and so the meeting depends upon the fidelity of the church to its dialectical vocation.

No task demands greater virtue than this, for in every community there is a deep xenophobic impulse that is no less strong when it goes unrecognized, an antipathy toward strangers that serves to cement the group together and to maintain its integrity. The alien is always a threat; his appearance intensifies our common interests against all other people. When the church is faithful to its mission, it also learns that its mission places its faith in grave jeopardy, simply because significant others now become strangers instead of familiar persons who affirm commitments that we all share. Nevertheless, there is no other way that the community can maintain faith with its own heritage, and so it is confronted with the mysterious involution of losing life and finding it once more. The lesson complements what the virtues themselves teach as they point toward sacrificial expressions of gratitude that they need not exemplify and cannot justify. The stranger is discussed most extensively in chapter 6.

In this sketch of the different virtues, there are several distinctive claims. Faith is equated with trust and loyalty toward whatever is found trustworthy. From our various faiths we derive images of the self and of its world, and these shape the way that we see, affording us a certain range of choice among different modes of conduct and precluding the choice of still other modes. We are men of many faiths; we cannot do without them no matter what they do with us, because the imagery that they provide is the only resource we have for the construction of individual and corporate identity. Pursuit of the "natural" virtues presupposes this sense of identity and its source in our faiths, else there is no "I" to begin the chase. If faith were not present, if it did not work with the love kindled from the love shown to us by others so that we could establish a realm of basic trust within which the self can test its powers and liberty, if hope did not counsel us to plan for tomorrow, we would have neither resources nor reason to seek what temperance or justice or courage requires. Consequently, the assumption that the "theological" virtues crown the "natural" should simply be stood on its head. Faith and hope and love are not some late and miraculous addition to existence, comforting and exhilarating but finally gratuitous. They are the indispensable foundation for everything else, the presuppositions as much as the goals of the quest for identity, as common as health and in other forms as prevalent as disease.

There are a number of arguments adduced in these pages against the distinction between natural and theological virtues, as well as against the conventional discrimination among "common" and "saving" forms of faith, hope, and love. In the end, we live with a tangle of faiths, and this essay offers no elaborate phenomenology that would attempt to sort out what we must acknowledge as inextricably unified, sometimes for the better and sometimes for the worse. The distinction between natural and theological, among its other deficiencies, has often been employed to argue that some virtues are achievements while others are gifts. In fact, however, we do not attain the "natural" virtues by our own un-aided efforts. Even the ingredients of autonomy have their real source beyond the self: so little do we have, indeed, that we have not received. The intention of *Faith and Virtue* is simply to anchor virtue in our common life, to display the dependence of the individual upon his communities and his achievements upon gifts from others, to show the ways in which each of the seven "cardinal" virtues is related to all the rest, and to defend the adequacy of this particular language to map some of the more obscure terrain of the moral landscape. If some conventional polarities are abandoned, I think that at least Aquinas would be sympathetic with the rejection of distinctions that were scarcely at the center of his own moral reflection and that were never employed there in the static and inflexible fashion in which they were used by others who have written more recently but less well.

There are several vocabularies at hand for the description of moral life, of course, and each of them offers its own distinctive contribution to whatever wisdom we accumulate about our humanness or lack of it. It would be rash to suggest that the language of virtue needs no complement and that reliance upon it means that we need not also speak of duties, obligations, and values. But at least it must not be ignored, for there is much to learn from its counsels about the importance of vision, the centrality of imagination, the exigencies of fair play, the involution of the moral and aesthetic aspects of life, the awesome power of habit, the dialectical impulses contained within the self, the different modalities of time, the significance of the stranger, and our dependence on what others do for us. Nor is there reason to identify the idea of virtue with a particular model of selfhood. By whatever approach we come to the mystery of becoming and being and betraying and retrieving what humanness means, virtue is relevant still.

In *The Age of the Person*, Dietrich von Oppen writes:

> If we are to master our world, it will not be along institutional lines or by institutional methods but primarily and especially through the person. We can no longer base our hopes on a system of regulations or on our awareness of such a system; on the contrary, we may expect pacification, reconciliation, and unity, if at all, only by virtue of the person. That means that we must seek a cure for our ills in an entirely different direction, since our own age has been trying to find its salvation by perfecting our social institutions and by planning our social system in ever greater detail.[3]

Perhaps von Oppen is too sanguine about the possibilities of the person to bend into new shape the structures of the social world; there are times when great patches of the reality we have constructed seem no longer amenable to humanization of any sort. But we are not distinguished from other animals because of the beauty or intricacy of our social order; we are different because within that order we have managed to preserve space for the individual to emerge. The self, not society, has been our particular contribution to the world. Frail though it is, the self is the only resource and the only justification and the only end that we have in the struggle to preserve what is most remarkably and peculiarly human. If we can continue to knit our future to our past and find any reason to be sanguine at all, we should not forget what the notion of virtue has to tell. That will not suffice, of course, for the knowledge of virtue is not so important as the practice of it. But it is a good place to begin.

PART ONE

1
habits

The language of virtue is not fashionable now, either in common discourse or within the Christian community. That may tell more about fashion than it does about virtue, less about the irrelevance of classical images than about the magnitude of contemporary hazards. Especially in times when individual agency appears to be a question more often than a certainty, when autonomy can be more surely predicated of systems than it can of persons, when the whole social fabric threatens to unravel, a sense of the seriousness of things grows impatient with the works of imagination and particularly with images like virtue that seem to reflect an age long gone. Its focus upon the growth of the individual appears profoundly anachronous when our corporate problems bulk so large, as though what it described were now conserved mainly in small New England villages for exhibit to the annual tourist trade. Even so, there is nothing alien to ourselves about either the meaning of the idea or the appetite to attain it, for what virtue denotes is simply human excellence, wholeness in the sense of the actualization of whatever possibilities our humanness enshrines. Certainly the ambition to achieve as much as we can of our potentialities can be phrased in many ways, although semantics are not unimportant. Each way is metaphorical, for wholeness cannot be found wherever existence has been flattened into prose. But if we rely entirely upon other images, it is possible that we will forget some truths that the language of virtue conveys better than other vocabularies can.

In the consciousness of the West, virtue has always been identified with habits. In the initially random mosaic of existence there appear some patterns that are reasonable and purposive, chosen by the self rather than forced upon it, maintained for the sake of fairness toward other people and not least of all toward oneself, and in these patterns we achieve what is most richly and distinctively human. The notion of virtue, then, begins by confronting us with one of the elemental realities of life: the pervasiveness of habit. There is nothing virtuous about everything habitual, of course, and habit is a dangerous adversary, one of the greatest of the principalities and powers of the world. Silent in its approach, subtle in its snares, brutal and brutalizing in its thousand tyrannies, it unmans its victims until they have neither will nor wisdom to seek escape. In its crimes there is none of the stuff of tragedy, not at first, for men lose themselves without knowledge either of how great the loss has been or even of the loss itself. After all, no face to which we are accustomed has vanished, no comfort been withdrawn; whatever anguish our repetitive and familiar ways sometimes arouse, is not this better than facing, without anodyne, the unknown? In *The Plague*, Albert Camus tells a story about habit—the habits that enforce alienation in the world of everyday, the new little ones that bar the door against anomie when the familiar world crumbles, the imperceptible but implacable return of the old when times of crisis pass. The scene is Oran, but every one of us has visited there and found himself no tourist but a resident in a land very much like home.

> The truth is that everyone is bored, and devotes himself to cultivating habits. . . . In the evening, on leaving the office, they foregather, at an hour that never varies, in the cafés, stroll the same boulevard, or take the air on their balconies. The passions of the young are violent and short-lived; the vices of older men seldom range beyond an addiction to bowling. . . . It will be said, no doubt, that these habits are not peculiar to our town; really all our contemporaries are much the same. . . . Nevertheless there still exist towns and countries where people have now and then an inkling of something different. In general it doesn't change their lives. Still, they have had an intimation, and that's so much to the good. Oran, however, seems to be a town without intimations; in other words, completely modern. Hence I see no need to dwell on the manner of loving in our town. The men and women consume one another rapidly in what is called "the act of love," or else settle down to a mild habit of conjugality. We seldom find a mean between these extremes. That, too, is not exceptional. At Oran, as elsewhere, for lack of time and thinking, people have to

love one another without knowing much about it. . . . But you can get through the days there without trouble, once you have formed habits. And since habits are precisely what our town encourages, all is for the best. Viewed from this angle, its life is not particularly exciting; that must be admitted. But, at least, social unrest is quite unknown among us. And our frank-spoken, amiable and industrious citizens have always inspired a reasonable esteem in visitors. Treeless, glamourless, soulless, the town of Oran ends by seeming restful and, after a while, you go complacently to sleep there.[1]

Often enough, an individual is victimized by the habits that he has developed before he is even aware of them; their hegemony constantly nibbles away the edges of his awareness of his own selfhood as well as his openness to others and to the world. No drug is more effective for those who want to drown every intimation and go "complacently to sleep." On the other hand, with the rest of the citizens of Oran we must cultivate habits to defend ourselves against anomie, against the completely paralyzing suspicion that there is no knot to the thread from which our common life is sewn. Then, too, we create habits in order to assert our identity against the routinization of life by the dictates of communities and powers greater than ourselves. We devise little strategies to persuade ourselves that the self has an independent life and is even enjoying itself, as a matter of fact, quite apart from the routinized world in which it is all consumptions and functions and roles. The strategies fail, as often as not, because they cannot transform or escape from the single modality of time that routinization establishes, time quantified, minutes without rightness or rhythm, measured by the clock and bleached. So we look for refuge in the habit of entertainment, hoping for a modest bit of ecstasy there that would be cheap at any price, but the play catches the conscience of no one and affords no new world to ingest the self. Instead, there is only a passive consumption of enjoyment that differs not at all from the obsession with consumption and passivity of everyday life. The cocktails and barbecues, the lawn and the walks, the camping and concerts, these too can become routine, increasing the mass of the everyday world they were intended to subvert.

Our problem, therefore, is not only the tyranny of bad habits but the way that very good ones dwindle to routine. Heritage is bastardized to convention by thoughtless and constant usage. The small gestures of daily life, devised in order to acknowledge the privacy and interiority and self-transcendence of the individual, end by depriving us of access to the realities they were intended to celebrate. A commonplace such as a handshake becomes a surrogate for what it was intended to inaugurate, a covert dismissal rather than a token of attentiveness and openness to the mystery of another creature who could address the self as "thou." Sometimes it is boredom, sometimes we know not what, sometimes a minor crisis, sometimes a sense of shame or incompletion in our transactions with another person that rekindles the appetite for ecstasy, for a new beginning, for standing outside the routinized self and all its habitual responses and ways of perceiving. Sometimes the everyday world provokes desperate and violent rebellion against itself, although such defiance cannot manage to escape its context; its violence, no less than the violence of our entertainments, is an extension of the fascination with power that lies at the heart of the everyday and supports its routinized ways.

The name of violent tactics for escape from the clutch of habit is *suddenness,* which Kierkegaard correctly described as an epiphany of the daimonic. The sudden is scarcely an instance of *kairos,* something accomplished at the right time, for it is tainted at its source, beginning as a gesture of recoil from what is less than human rather than as a reaching toward what is fully so. Far from hopeful, it really testifies that there are no grounds for hope at all, no reason to counsel patience, no benign rhythm written into the structure of time. Rebellion is as sterile as submission; neither one is able to envision, much less achieve, a transformation of the quality of life. What marks the sudden as not simply impotent but daimonic is its refusal to acknowledge the temporal conditions of creatureliness, its confusion of the human with a spurious image of the divine. The self lives in time and time lives within the self, shaping its present possibilities in accordance with the legacy of its past; so the sudden can do nothing except briefly interrupt the rule of habits or else establish itself as a new one, far more dangerous than the old. Patterns still emerge, of course, but now in a random way; constants remain but they are not trustworthy simply because they are constant, for now they exist to indulge the endless passion for novelty and distraction. Instinct and desire dispose of a self that is even less at its own disposal than it was before.

Habit is never vanquished. Instead, new ones simply preclude some of the best of the old—visiting an aged aunt, playing a familiar game, gentleness toward an odd neighborhood child. Sometimes it seems as though we cannot do with habits and we cannot do without them. With them we purchase some measure of alienation and without them we drift toward anomie. The nature of the self is such, however, that it cannot be other than a creature of habit. The real question never concerns how the world of habit can be overcome, as though it were a realm of inauthenticity; such transcendence would deprive us of ourselves. The problem has to do with the humanization of habit, with the cultivation of those that will serve to distinguish our actions from the ways of all other animals and express what is most rigorously and completely human, and with the rejuvenation of habit so that convention becomes heritage again.

There are many ways to approach the moral life, and none can stand alone; among them, the language of value and the vocabulary of duty offer their special contributions to the sum that we can learn about what it means to be human. The notion of virtue incorporates something of what these other ways of speaking suggest; fair play, for example, is a value and a matter of duty or obligation no less than it is the substance of what the virtues counsel. What is most interesting is the relationship among them all, and not the question of whether one can be regarded as primary. The particular virtue of the notion of virtue, however, lies in all that it has to say about time and vision. Seeing is as arduous as it is crucial for moral life, because vision is the real architect of our decisions. In its emphasis upon the importance of imagination and in its focus upon the integral relationship between the moral and aesthetic aspects of our lives, the idea of virtue can provide some remedy for our manipulative and instrumental approach to the world and its populace. Equally important, its consistent concern with the problem of time and with the development of habit might even remind a society which has lost its sense of rhythm that there is more to reality than the present moment, greater rewards than instant gratification, higher values than relevance to the contemporary scene.

Virtue teaches that the moment holds more than itself and that nowhere will we find a world without consequences. In our contemporary American cult of youth the moment is severed from past and future both, so that we deny any rhythm to the course of time, find no reason to husband and cultivate talents for the future, discover no resources to sustain us if we should ever grow old. Trust no one over thirty. Of all the sins, the worst is to grow old, when flesh hangs pendulous from shrunken arms that once could bend the world to their will, when the face is distorted into the likeness of a fish by the frenzy of the lungs to prolong a useless life. We evade the acknowledgment of our frailty and death until the realities are upon us, only then to discover how great the strength and wisdom that our evasion has cost. Within the precincts of the idol of youth lies the most fertile soil for the growth of intolerance and indifference toward anything not intimately related to the appetites of the self. The misapprehension of temporality is the greatest of our illusions, and the worst correlate of belief that the moment is all is the assumption of a world without consequences in which only the most unlucky will ever have to pay. Deprivation will excuse or permissiveness affirm or affluence offer compensation for any sort of crime. Trial marriages are a paradigm of the brave new world in which everyone is invited to fly now, pay later—if ever, unless it did not happen to qualify as a business expense.

All of this seems to find some justification in the peculiarly American myth of the new beginning: we are the citizens of a new world. There is a frontier to the West where one need not pay for old mistakes or for the mistakes of older men. Life begins at forty. This is the first day of the rest of your life. But the illusion collides with the wiser biblical story of man's fall and impotence to heal himself: "the good that I would, I do not; but the evil which I would not, that I do (Rom. 7:19, KJV)." There are few consequences of our actions from which we can escape, and that is why Tarrou is correct in *The Plague* when he numbers first among habits the necessity for "unremitting vigilance." Perhaps money or prestige will save us from public consequences, but there is much truth in the classical dictum that one who injures is more to be pitied than the one who is injured, because of the rot that the first man is carefully nurturing in the chambers of the heart.

In "The Bear," William Faulkner writes of the initiation of a boy to virtue—to pity and fairness and friendship, "the will and hardihood to endure and the humility and skill to survive . . . the virtues of cunning and strength and speed."[2] These prizes are integrally bound up with the vanishing forest, "bigger and older than any recorded document:—of white man fatuous enough to believe he had bought any fragment of it, of Indian ruthless enough to pretend that any fragment of it had been his to convey," and especially with "the ancient and unremitting contest according to the ancient and immitigable rules"[3] that is played in the wilderness each year by Ike McCaslin and his friends. The annual hunt is less a quest for game than a celebration of an ageless bear called Old Ben, who in some mysterious fashion is the "epitome and apotheosis of the old wild life."[4] Through this "yearly pageant-rite of the old bear's furious immortality"[5] Ike comes to maturity, eventually managing to make his own what had been "his heritage but not yet his patrimony."[6] When he is twenty-one, Ike recognizes that "his novitiate to the true wilderness"[7] has prepared him —and, indeed, constrains him—to relinquish the plantation that he has inherited. He sees its history as part and paradigm of the universal history recorded in the biblical tale of creation and fall, the story of man's ineradicable passion to pretend that he holds absolute power of disposal over the heart of the wilderness and the wilderness of the heart that both belong ultimately only to God. To his cousin, McCaslin Edmonds, Ike says:

> The five hundred years of absentee landlords in the Roman bagnios, and the thousand years of wild men from the northern woods who dispossessed them and devoured their ravished substance ravished in turn again and then snarled in what you call the old world's worthless twilight over the old world's gnawed bones, blasphemous in His name until He used a simple egg to discover to them a new world where a nation of people could be founded in humility and pity and sufferance and pride of one to another. . . . He ordered and watched it. He saw the land already accursed even as Ikkemotubbe and Ikkemotubbe's father old Issetibbeha and old Issetibbeha's fathers too held it, already tainted even before any white man owned it by what Grandfather and his kind, his fathers, had brought into the new land which He had vouchsafed them out of pity and sufferance, on condition of pity and humility and sufferance and endurance, from that old world's corrupt and worthless twilight as though in the sailfuls of the old world's tainted wind which drove the ships—[8]

We will never have a new beginning because we must carry into the future what we have been, no new worlds because their citizens will be ourselves, no new landscapes because the shadow of our selfishness falls across every perspective, no actions without consequences because the old is contained in the new and the new is held within the egg of the old. But if we have less than that, we also have more. "The Bear" draws us into a new world that affords a structure of temporality within which the cultivation of virtue is possible even though arduous. There is a ritual that can bring a child the clarification of moral vision which is the presupposition of virtue, and with its attainment there becomes possible a climactic act of renunciation in which the self grasps and affirms the meaning and worth of being a man. Childless, Isaac McCaslin eventually becomes "Uncle Ike" to half a county, much as Old Ben, "Priam reft of his old wife and outlived all his sons,"[9] midwived the manhood of Ike and provisioned him with a patrimony far greater than any heritage that could be written on paper by a lawyer's hand.

No other vocabulary for the moral life insists so strongly upon the cruciality of time, which offers every individual opportunities for growth and development because it has an incremental and rhythmic character and is much more than random succession. On the other hand, time can ravage the self, for it is much less than a series of *kairoi*. Moments rich with intimations and challenges are always rare and men must arm themselves to manage the self and its affairs during the long and tedious reigns of *kronos*, when time is splintered and flat and quantified. Neither every hour nor every generation is equally close to eternity. Because time abides within the self, man is accountable for himself, agent as well as patient, project as well as response. The way that the self responds today to what is visited upon it shapes the sort of self that will be able to respond tomorrow, augments or plunders whatever resources there will be to domesticate its visitors in the future. How we respond to the external depends upon the emergent shape we have given to the internal, and transformation of whatever lies within ourselves becomes ever more difficult as the inheritance of the past increases by daily increments, each imperceptible but together a weight that simply overwhelms our modest strength. The project of selfhood may be accomplished thoughtlessly, in ways that are brutal and coarse, but the crux of the matter is not what is visited upon the self but how it has used its time to habituate itself to listen, to see, to answer the knocks at its door.

The role of the self in its own creation, rarely as much chosen as it is simply enforced by our temporality, is one aspect of the involution of our moral and aesthetic lives. In every individual there reside certain potentialities that could never be realized except by this single and singular existent, this odd I who brings a unique genetic endowment and a unique history to situations that can never be repeated, just because of the involvement of this individual within them. In the realization of these possibilities that can never be entirely duplicated, the self has its own opportunity, shared with no one else at all, to contribute to the diversity and enrichment of the realm of the actual, and by that act to honor and acknowledge what is supremely actual, God. So the self is called to live for itself as well as for others and, indeed, to live for itself if it is to be able to live fully for others. He who does not possess himself can scarcely offer himself to others; nor by attempting to offer what one does not possess will one find a sufficient strategy to gain possession of the citadel of one's own selfhood.

The most important aspect of this involution, however, concerns the question of vision. When persons act in different ways, we are quick to give some unflattering label to their conduct because we are reluctant to accept behavior alien to our own. But this sort of evaluation does nothing to penetrate the mystery of why they act as they do. The core of that mystery is simply that different people see the world differently. We live not only in the gray and largely undifferentiated continuum of a public world in which subservience to certain conventions is expected of us all, but also in many and various private worlds, some twisted and labyrinthine and anchored in the cellarage of the mind, others invested with the dazzling simplicity that is fathered by obsession. Our worldly ways reflect the world as we see it; we are free to act in some purposive fashion only within the world that we can see. Before our decisions, supporting our approach to moral life, distinguishing us from our neighbors, there is our way of seeing. But it is not easy to see, no easier than it is to listen, to hear not what we would like, not what we would expect, not only what the language means, but what intention and anguish and hope are veiled as well as disclosed by the recalcitrance of words. Seeing is never simply a reaction to what passes before our eyes; it is a matter of how well the eye is trained and provisioned to discern the richness and the terror, beauty and banality, of the worlds outside and within the self.

Decisions are shaped by vision, and the ways that we see are a function of our "character," of the history and habits of the self, and ultimately of the stories that we have heard and with which we identify ourselves. More precisely—to anticipate a later chapter—seeing is determined by the constellation of images of man and the world that resides within the household of the self. Sometimes they inhibit and corrupt a person as much as they sustain him, but their common source is always faith, the tangle of loyalties that the self has developed in the course of time. Because our faiths are little less than innumerable, many dwelling uneasily together within a single self, the worlds that men inhabit are enough to furnish a whole new galaxy. The real problem, however, is not the variety of faiths we entertain or images of man by which we are all beset, nor their partiality, nor even the conflicts among them, but our need for a master image of the self that can reconcile the lesser ones that draw a person first one way and then another toward conflicting goals, each of them claiming greater authority than it deserves, promising greater rewards than it can provide.

The master image that is particularly congruent with the notion of virtue and that brings to moral vision some of the clarity we need is the figure of the player. Play has always been one of the primary means of socialization in the West, for it invites the child to test his agency, to create a new time that interrupts the rule of *kronos,* to create a special place of his own ordered by imagination, and to acknowledge the importance of fairness in relationships with others as well as toward himself. But playing is much more than an apprenticeship in virtue. Faith, hope, and love have traditionally been described as "effects of grace" insofar as they are born from and sustained by the disclosure of the holy. The first implicate of this revelation for man's understanding of himself is a perspective at once penitent and "unserious." After all, the disclosure of that which alone is ultimately serious renders everything else unserious in comparison. The presence of God means judgment upon the seriousness—or cynicism, which is just seriousness in twisted form—with which we hitherto regarded all our own strengths and weaknesses, relationships and achievements. The price of the illusion that we are our own gods is a spirit of unremitting self-seriousness, for then there is no power to assist us, no way to retrieve a lost moment, no court of appeal. But the disclosure of the holy liberates man to grasp the dialectic of his freedom from the world as well as his responsibilities toward it. The image of the player recognizes the tentative and provisional character of all our serious concerns while still affirming the importance of order and discipline. In a sense, then, the man who believes himself to be a child of God is freed to revert to the spirit of childhood play, although now with a new maturity that is able to comprehend the integral relationship between self-denial and self-fulfillment, sacrifice and victory.

At the same time, the common concern of what have usually been called the "natural" virtues—temperance, justice, courage, and prudence—is with playing fair, fairness toward all other selves and not least toward the wholeness of one's own self. The "theological" virtues, therefore, are bound up with the gift of a master image of man that provides final justification for the fair playing to which the "natural" virtues individually and together call him. In their different ways, the "natural" virtues expand the significance of play and provide concrete images that enable men to act in particular situations in ways that are faithful to this new understanding of the self. In their shared focus upon playing and the player lies the secret of the unity of the virtues natural and theological. This unity and the dependence of all the virtues upon one another demonstrate that, in its most profound and expansive sense, playing is not an achievement of one's own as much as it is a gift from others, not a project of the self as much as the consequence of the caring of parents and peers and of the condescension of God. The image of the player is most important, however, not because it obligates us to the principle of fairness but because of its direct consequences for our vision. On the one hand, it counsels against obsession with and fixation upon any single fact which then becomes a *daimon* because it is not relativized and qualified by its context. This sort of neurotic seriousness is never congruent with playing. On the other, it establishes empathetic regard, because everyone is at least potentially a player in the same game. So the image structures vision in a way that fulfills the two fundamental requisites for clarity of sight: it offers us the sort of perspective that keeps daimons at bay and the imaginative sensitivity that carries us beneath the surfaces of reality.

It is true, of course, that the revelation of the holy finally calls into question the whole notion of virtue, just as it questions everything else that man is or has devised. Revelation testifies that man's alienation will never be overcome by the achievement of virtue, for it is ingredient in every heroic act, in the most strenuous play, in the finest essays of the imagination. But that is a matter for the end of the story; in the beginning, it is better not to dismiss the idea in the name of a higher wisdom, at least not until we have made our own whatever assistance the image can afford. We begin, then, with the knowledge that existence is a mosaic of habits and that the passage of time exerts awesome power within us all. Our problem is the humanization of habit: the rescue of those that have dwindled to mere conventionalities until they are luminous with heritage again, the celebration of those that will permit the self to express its wholeness rather than fall into slavery to anxiety about the future, and a commitment to those that enable us to play fairly with other selves and so, in the end, with our own selves as well. Behind the actions that habit dictates there is the vision of self and world that induces habit and that habits confirm, a way of seeing that imagination has devised and that faith and love sustain. Vision depends upon images and finally upon a master image, and all our imagery is awarded to us by faith. Among our many faiths, at least Christian versions can provide the master image of the player, and this can remedy the principal defects from which our vision suffers. These contentions need elaboration and defense, of course, but one thing is certain. The mystery of why we see the world as we do provides the best evidence that an old affirmation about some of the virtues is valid still—Paul's claim that "faith, hope, love abide, these three."

2
seeing

The idea of the holy and the language of virtue were born and grew up on opposite shores of the Mediterranean. It has often been argued that they represent approaches to the nature of the self that cannot be reconciled. H. Richard Niebuhr, for one, comments:

> When the ethical reflections of Scripture are systematized with the aid of ideas developed by Greco-Roman-Western reason, considerable violence is done to them and the way is opened to many misconceptions and malpractices. . . . That is to say, the idea of virtue itself has no real place in Christian ethics. If we continue to use it, as it seems almost necessary to do, since we have no other word for the gifts which have personal conduct as their matter, we must always do it with the qualification that we mean by it neither achievement nor habit, but gift and response.[1]

Niebuhr is skeptical of the idea because he understands it to regard as an achievement what is really a gift, to confuse habits with what are actually fruits of relationships that depend upon the presence of other selves, and to ignore other patterns of behavior that can claim to be "theological virtues" just as legitimately as can faith, hope, and love. Certainly there is little sense in speaking of faith in God as though it were a "rational habit." Often enough, our faiths and loves are responses as volatile and contingent as the relationships with other persons that elicit them.

Even so, when faith, hope, and love are traced to their roots in the experiences of childhood, it seems an error to juxtapose relationship and habit or gift and achievement. The virtues are neither one nor the other as much as they are both. A child begins to love in response to the love he has received quite apart from any striving or deserving of his own; he learns to trust only after the trustworthiness of his surroundings has been mediated to him by all sorts of small parental acts. The magnitude of our capacity to respond to others and to the world is awarded to us, not innate and not earned but given by what other persons do. On the other hand, the gift of the power of promise-making and promise-keeping does not continue to depend upon the presence of the family; it is internalized as habit that shapes our ordinary commerce with reality after these significant others are with us no more. The gifts foster the growth of habit and the habit discloses the significance of the gifts. Were it not for the caring of others, the habit would not be ours; but it is our own achievement now, a sign of independence, a commitment that we have chosen to honor and maintain not only among family and friends but wherever we go.

Nevertheless, for reasons other than the ones that Niebuhr mentions, "theological virtues" is an expression more venerable than satisfactory. Not only will it become evident later that the distinction between "theological" and "natural" virtues is a misconstruction, there are also some difficulties involved in the usage of "theological" at all in this context. From a Christian perspective, these virtues certainly do not counsel men to turn away from the world in search of some other place whose resident is more worthy of devotion than the populace of the earth. Instead, no matter whether common or Christian, they are born in the course of man's most ordinary and inescapable commerce with his environment, nurtured as that commerce grows more intense and profound, and become genuinely theological when an individual finds intimations of the presence of the holy in the detail of the finite and definite. They are theological, in other words, simply because they emerge from the human and draw man more deeply into it, for this is the only path that leads to the divine. The eyes of faith look nowhere except to the natural for the sight of grace and glory.

It is dangerous to characterize faith or hope or love as resolutely theological because this tends to invest them with a purity that in fact is never there and suggests that they float somewhere beyond the tumult and welter of our absorptions with the self, far from our shifting allegiances and conflicting appetites. But faith that can be identified with explicit religious commitment is always entangled with other varieties of itself, common and pervasive. The disclosure of the holy in Jesus Christ judges and condemns the idolatrous forms of our common faiths, and yet the loyalty and trust engendered by revelation are ensnarled with them still. Christian commitment, then, is not so much another brand of faith that displaces earlier versions as counterpoint to the melody and dissonance of the rest of them, a note of *metanoia,* a sort of penitence that mysteriously adds a deeper resonance to their hoping in its judgment on their hope. But our concatenation of loyalties and adventures in trust, those maintained as well as others disappointed and betrayed, not only diverts us from the possibility of more expansive commitments; they also point, at least in oblique ways, toward what is greater than themselves. After all, the analogies between ordinary experience and Christian proclamation are what render the latter an intelligible and significant option. The continuities among our different faiths and hopes and loves, as much as the magnitude of the judgment that revelation enforces upon their everyday expressions, are what challenge the self to accept a new mode of existence. We live with a tangle of faiths; no attempt to discriminate among their "common" and "saving" forms will quite manage to sort and sift what we know, sometimes sadly enough, as inextricably involved with one another.

But the greatest difficulty with the notion of "theological virtue" is not its unwarranted imputation of purity so much as its entirely erroneous suggestion that there is something extraordinary and rare about the presence of faith, hope, and love. These are the commonest of all human phenomena, familiar as laughter or hunger or sleep, and they inform every significant relationship whatsoever with other selves, communities, institutions, and with the earth itself. Being with others inaugurates new possibilities, and these kindle new hopes that the self could scarcely entertain when it was alone. The caring of others conveys to children a sense of their own identity and its special worth, tutoring them in the sort of regard for the self without which we can never genuinely love other selves. Family and friends elicit the trust and loyalty that are the primary ingredients of faith, their presence establishing a realm of basic trust within which the child is free to test his powers, dare to dream, risk a fall.

Without faith in the self and trust in a certain orderliness within the context of the self, it is impossible to plan for tomorrow. If there is no reason to hope that the world will prove amenable to our actions, if all our projects are really hopeless, we are robbed of tomorrow and consigned to a dreary land where there is nothing for which to hope except the certainty of death. If the caring of others has not born in us some modicum of love for our own particular humanity, as well as for theirs and for the earth that sustains us together, no motive remains for anything at all. Where these virtues do not flourish, neither will life endure. The elemental necessities for life everywhere, always, and for all, are a certain love for one's self, faith in the world, hope for tomorrow. The conviction that virtue in this rude form can sometimes develop into Christian commitment must not blunt recognition that these three are as universal as health and, in still other forms, as common as sickness. They are present whenever a decision is made or a game is played, wherever there is a birthday party or a child smiles or a woman combs her hair before going out. "So faith, hope, love abide, these three"—Paul's familiar statement can serve not only as an expression of the Christian vision but equally well as an empirical generalization. Sometimes their dimensions are very modest, their shape twisted and difficult to recognize; even so, they are with us still.

No other "habit" has the same primacy and importance that belong to these three, for they are the source of our way of seeing, presiding over vision and its vicissitudes just as vision sustains and refines each of them in a movement of constant reciprocity. *Faith interprets, love unites, hope creates.* Each has its own task, its distinct identity, and yet it depends entirely upon the health of the others. More than that, hope is exactly what it is and nothing else, and yet it would not be hope if love and faith were not contained within it, just as it is always contained within each of them. With the loss of one, all are lost. Niebuhr correctly recognizes that:

> Without love and faith hope is empty, or does not exist at all. Each of the virtues has its distinctive character, but none of them can be in action without the others. The danger, of course, of every analysis of Christian life is that the distinction of various aspects will lead to the thought that it is a union of parts and this may lead to the mistaken effort to add virtue to virtue. Hence it is intelligible why at various times the effort to do justice to the unity of Christian life should have led to the effort to concentrate it in one of the virtues as the source and bearer of all the rest. So

faith in the days of the Reformation, love in the time of liberalism and now hope, has been regarded as the fundamental, or the original or the key virtue. However, none of these is the key to or the foundation of the others. . . . They constitute a unity and not a collection of responses or virtues. They cannot be added to each other so that one of them might be possible to the self without the other two.[2]

Their inseparability reflects their common source in the life of the imagination, which must not be relegated to some odd corner in the recesses of the self, as though it were a special faculty or something esoteric. Imagination is not a refuge from the "serious business" of life but the source of the concrete images of the world and of the individual as agent in the world, without which there could be no serious business at all. It is intended to feed on actuality, not illusion, and the gauge of its health is how greatly it prefers any scrap of the real world to the finest fantasy. When it finds among the scraps some intimation of the holy, the supremely actual, imagination is healed in the sense that its doors are thrown open to more of the realm of the actual than they would hitherto admit. The sick imagination that was running from a world too much for it is turned around, lured away from the isolation it had temporarily chosen by the dazzle of what sustains everything that is.

Where love is absent, what has occurred is mainly a paralysis of the imagination, a clouding of vision, an inability to bring before the eye of the mind all the weight and specificity, all the strangenesses and incongruities, of another human being. Love cannot win its struggle to be born until the self pauses and allows imagination to clothe with flesh the shadow of a stranger. Sometimes the heart is filled with terror or hatred of another self instead of love. Then imagination has been gutted by the sort of fixation that separates one trait or incident from its human context, from the freckled hand that acted or the hair fallen across the eye that watched or the small muscle inside the chest that beat its accompaniment to the act. One event is abstracted from the history of the self, or an individual history is abstracted from the history of the community of which it is a part, and then everything is interpreted in the false brilliance of obsession with this particular that, in its isolation, has become a *daimon*, filling the whole horizon. Perspective is lost and everything falls out of relation, as

though there were no magnetism able to draw together the dis-
orderly filings of life. No less than love, hope is also a child of
imagination, imaging and ordering the world of the possible,
sketching a future where hitherto there was only a past, turning
from a path that leads nowhere in order to imagine a better way
and, by imagining, sometimes to create the possibility for which it
hoped.

In *Images of Hope,* William F. Lynch describes the imagination, simply but accurately, as

> the sum total of all the forces and faculties in man that are brought
> to bear upon our concrete world to form proper images of it. The
> first task of such an imagination, if it is to be healing, is to find a
> way through fantasy and lies into fact and existence. The second
> task of such an imagination is to create perspectives for the facts
> it has found. It will refuse to leave facts as scattered absolutes, to
> preoccupy and frighten human beings.[3]

If imagination is to find a way through fantasy and lies into fact
and existence, it must be companioned by the love that unites men
with the realities of their world, the faith that interprets experience so that truth is not confused with fantasies that threaten to
preoccupy and frighten people, and the hope that creates new
possibilities instead of yielding to the dictates of scattered absolutes. These twin challenges that confront imagination, the challenges of empathetic regard and synthesizing perspectives, are
given at least partial resolution by the master image of play and
the player. The discovery of the facts and the provision of perspectives upon them are different or surely distinguishable tasks,
and for each of them we rely at first upon different resources even
though, in the end, they are bound up inseparably with one another.

On the one hand, our commerce with facts is mediated by our
images of the world. Man is not a camera and does not number
among his possessions any sense that could be titled "the naked
eye." Vision depends upon and elaborates images of the world
that are the legacy of our past and distillations of the stories that
we have heard. When he argues that the patterns of behavior of
every organism are determined by a constellation of imagery,
Kenneth Boulding describes these images of the world as fields
suffused with values that draw the attention and activity of the

self toward whatever is seen as most valuable of all. Between the messages that the self transmits and the ones that it receives, he comments in *The Image,* "lies the great intervening variable of the image. The outgoing messages are the result of the image, not the result of the incoming messages. The incoming messages only modify the outgoing messages as they succeed in modifying the image."[4] Communications from others and impressions of the world, then, have the power to change our accustomed ways only insofar as they manage to transform our symbolic universe, constraining us to rearrange the dense and multifaceted picture of the world that we have previously devised.

But we encounter great difficulties now, for the relationship between our experience and our familiar imagery of the world is a complex and untrustworthy one. New facts are not admitted to consciousness free of charge. Their significance is sometimes rejected and much more often disguised by valuational schemes that are already resident in our particular symbolic universe. In other words, our perspective does far less than justice to the facts; instead of relating them to one another it simply refuses to provide any lodging at all for the ones that are not congruent with itself. We shrink from challenges too arduous, intimations too threatening, from whatever promises to overturn familiar expectations, and we find a thousand ways to resist perceptions that conflict with our established structure of values. Perspective struggles against fact and its frequent victories testify that it is lord more often than servant of our image of the world. Boulding correctly perceives that:

> Even at the level of simple or supposedly simple sense perception we are increasingly discovering that the message which comes through the senses is itself mediated through a value system. We do not perceive our sense data raw; they are mediated through a highly learned process of interpretation and acceptance. . . . What this means is that for any individual organism or organization, there are no such things as "facts." There are only messages filtered through a changeable value system.[5]

It is true, of course, that certain "facts" smash through whatever defenses we have erected for the protection of our particular image of things—the enervation that age brings, the death of someone we have loved, a gesture of indifference or impatience that tears apart our world like an earthquake because it comes from where once we looked for greatest assurance and support. Were this not possible, no sense could be made of the disclosure of the holy when God appears in order to judge the human and rapture it beyond itself. Even so, "the way in which the total image grows determines or at least limits the directions of future growth,"[6] as Boulding notes, and it is perspective rather than the accumulation of new facts, even those so overwhelming that they dictate much of the way they must be perceived, that determines the growth of the image. The authority of habits, the comforts of familiar conventions, the complex reality that we roughly describe by the word "character"—all these reinforce the power of yesterday to legislate what it is that we can see today and how much else there is that we shall never manage to bring into focus and find a way to confront.

Where do we gain our perspectives? The bundle of loves or valuational scheme that resides within our picture of the world, barricading the doors against some facts while it reaches out to welcome others, finally depends upon how we envision our own selves, our nature and possibilities and limitations. It is this baggage of images of the self that furnishes the different perspectives upon the world that decide what we shall and shall not see. We view the world from the standpoint of the self and, indeed, there is no other way for us to see it. In a sense, this is to say that man is ineradicably selfish and that his selfishness blurs and warps his vision of everything else. On the other hand, these images involve loves and loyalties that lure the self far out beyond the counsels of its own selfishness and enforce upon it standards of trustworthiness that demand all sorts of self-denial and self-sacrifice. In other words, our point of view is not simply an "epistemological datum" or evidence of our fallenness; it is also an achievement and a pledge, the mark of our individuality. Images of the world and images of the self constantly influence one another, of course, for each is inevitably ingredient in the other. It is the imagery of the self that an individual holds, however, not his picture of the world, that is the most important architect of conduct; no matter where the most exciting lures and challenging values are believed to reside, one must image and envision oneself in pursuit of them if that pursuit is ever to begin. When the taste of the world has soured and there seems nothing new under the sun, the root of our impoverishment is the loss of an image of the self that can incite a person to plunge again into the midst of things.

The source of our imagery of selfhood, and therefore of our perspectives, always lies in faith, some of the meanings of which are *fiducia,* or trust, and loyalty toward whatever is found trustworthy.[7] Faith is occasioned and nourished by all the care a child finds lavished upon himself and by the consistency of his own small world, or else by whatever surrogates for parental love he stumbles upon in the streets if he has missed what most other children have. Then it gains new dimensions through transactions with peers and figures of authority outside the home, although in this larger world old securities also erode. From these relationships of trust and loyalty, no matter how tainted they are by incontrovertible evidence of promises broken as often as they are kept and by frequent misunderstandings as well as fidelity, we derive our enduring pictures of ourselves. The commerce of a person with his own body and with his immediate environment, with family and friends, with school and nation and values institutionalized in many and diverse ways—from all of this we garner perspectives that are imbedded in the images of the self that the relationships provide. The achievement of identity is an imaginative act, something rather precarious that we build from a great bunch of images that are the reflections and consequences of our trusting and our keeping of trust.

It is an error, then, to identify faith with belief or to equate it with explicit religious commitment. Nevertheless, the old scholastic notion of faith as *assensus,* assent to revealed truth, comes close to something of what faith involves: it is the source of our way of envisioning the self, and so of our way of seeing the world. The bundle of loves that determines our own particular way of seeing things, and therefore determines what we can hope for and want to hope for, depends upon the faith that informs a whole tangle of relationships with other selves, communities, and institutions. So, once again, in the exploration of our ways of seeing there is evidence that always "faith, hope, love abide, these three." Images shape our vision and dictate our conduct, and they are the offspring of faith—but not of faith alone. This is a particularly important instance of the way that faith, hope, and love, despite different identities, are each contained within the others.

Some of our images of the self conflict with others, none is more than partial, more than a few claim a total allegiance in certain circumstances that is scarcely congruent with the limited aspects of the self that they include, others twist and narrow our perspectives, still more threaten us with the sort of alienation that reduces a man to nothing except functions and roles. Sometimes one of them is dominant, sometimes another, each awarded temporary supremacy by the exigencies of the situation or the flights of fantasy. More often than not, then, we are many selves instead of one, a succession rather than a constant, many parts but never a whole. If the individual is ever to escape the phantasmagoria of his selves, or slavery to a part of himself that suppresses the legitimate ambitions of other parts, release will come only by way of the emergence of a master image that can dominate its situation, amplify and rectify our vision. The more rich and expansive that image, of course, the more options existence will offer to the self, for our real possibilities will not surpass our imaginative grasp of what existence contains for us—although our opportunities can obviously be far less than we imagine them. But our faiths are many and various and mercurial, fattening and waning with no particular rhythm. None seems able to discipline the rest. Some endure in one form or another, while others are ephemeral as twilight. Some diminish the self as much as others enrich it. Sometimes betrayal and disloyalty have their corrosive ways with them until the self is suspicious of faith itself. So the one image that is the end of our quest continues to elude us. We cannot do without our faiths, however, for without them we have nowhere to turn in order to harvest the small images from which identity is built and prisms are fashioned so that we can see our world. But vision naturally reaffirms the faiths that shaped its particular way of seeing, salvaging them from the jeopardy in which their own ambiguities and incompleteness have placed them.

If we are ever to achieve or even to understand the sort of human excellence that metaphors for moral life were minted to express, the focus of our reflection must shift from acts to images, from agency to vision, from the external to the internal, from choice and decision to the question of perspectives, from "practical reason" to the life of the imagination. It is the virtue of the idea of virtue to stress these concerns and to insist that the meaning of our humanity can be glimpsed more profoundly in the development of small habits than in occasional heroics, that it is more clearly manifest in the consistency and depth of a point of view than in sudden gestures of sacrifice or charity. Stanley Hauerwas comments wisely upon the deficiencies of our contemporary understanding of personality, which he believes

> has implied that men can be free as they choose, creating their values in relation to an easily comprehensible empirical world. It has failed to note that moral change and achievement are slow, for it has wanted to create the impression that we can change our moral self through the process of choice. But we are not free in the sense of being able suddenly to alter ourselves since we cannot alter what we can see and thus what we desire and are compelled by.[8]

There is only a single resource for those who are determined to alter how they see, and therefore what they will see and what they can be. That is the imagination, and its instrument is the image. But what we require is, in the end, precisely what we cannot provide for ourselves. Images depend on our relationships with others, and these involve not only reciprocity but often an initiative beyond our own and incommensurate with anything we deserve or can inspire. The continuation of these relationships demands gestures of reconciliation that we cannot effect without assistance, but our life together has often deprived others of any reason to come to our aid. The world as we know it sometimes seems to summon all its powers to despoil our humanness. In the best of times we are strangely vulnerable and, often enough, we hurry to join the world's conspiracy. Even when we do not venture beyond the charmed circles of family and peers, confidences meet indifference, anguish finds incomprehension, trust is repulsed. So imagination is impoverished because it dwells in a fallen world. Our transactions with others and with ourselves stifle a way of seeing that could justify the pursuit of virtue or preside over the emergence of a master image such as the one of man as player which could marshal all the powers of the individual in devotion to the meaning of fair play.

It is precisely this lack of justification for the image that furnishes the best reason for its adoption. This does not involve merely an invitation to arbitrariness, but if the fallenness of self and world deprives imagination of the nourishment for which it hungers, there is no cure for its enervation except a new perspective that can qualify and relativize the seriousness with which we have hitherto regarded the raptures and ravages of life, its tedium and coarseness and confusion and wonder. We need the sort of perspective that can dissolve all the scattered absolutes in the world and counsel in every situation: "This is not all." But we need more, too, for our perspective must not regard with ultimate seriousness even the whole concatenation of things that comprise the human situation—including, not least of all, the validity of our own point of view. It must be sufficiently expansive, then, to address some great and hitherto undigested lumps of living and press from them some of their ambiguities and complexity, so that we will not ever celebrate uncritically or damn absolutely the earth and its society.

The images of play and of man as player can fashion a point of view that will liberate imagination from some of the consequences of its fallen nature and context, offering a perspective that will enable life to continue, no matter how bleak it sometimes seems, but that will not bind us to pursuit of the continuation of life at any price, no matter how splendid it sometimes appears. This imagery can represent the conclusions of cynicism or indifference, of course, as well as express the commitments and affirm the autonomy of the individual. Certainly the ambiguities and contradictions of our actual experience provide no firm mandate whatsoever for reliance upon it in order to understand the self and establish its point of view. Nevertheless, the image of the player is deeply congruent with the Christian vision and lies at the heart of the whole idea of virtue; finally, there is no justification except one variety of faith or another for anything at all.

The Christian vision is no more than one way of seeing among a great many, and there is no reason to adopt this particular point of vantage except the obvious one—belief that the imagery on which it relies will introduce us most fully and meticulously to the realm of the actual, dissolving the daimonism of scattered absolutes because of its witness to the reality that alone is supremely actual. These images have a certain indeterminate and open quality, as the figures of playing and the player suggest, so that instead of leading the self toward a new form of alienation they lure men to the achievement of their own autonomy and prepare them to offer their own distinctive contributions to the increase of actuality. A rough mode of verification of the Christian vision, indeed, lies precisely in the way that the openness of these images toward the free development of the human is combined with the cogency and concreteness they offer for deciphering intimations of the divine. It is true that men often do not act in ways that are faithful to the images they have received; there is sickness as well as health in everyone. Even so, the images themselves retain a richness of meaning that can eventually subvert the arbitrary and exclusive points of view they are frequently utilized to maintain. Then, too, they are a shared legacy, remembered and valued by many, and the ways in which they are used by others, and lived by others, can sometimes shatter the hardness of one's own heart and turn imagination back toward more of the actual again.

Christian faith, in other words, does not mean faith in a god who is peculiarly the property of Christians. Instead, it means that the ways in which the commonwealth of man is related to the holy are brought into focus through a certain constellation of myths, images, symbols, and stories that are found primarily within the historical Christian community, although not there alone. So faith involves the imagination working to order experience in the context of this tradition, exploring the detail of individual existence for whatever witness to the holy it contains. Faith is not faith in images, of course, but without them there is no way that men can find faithful access to the divine. As the deposit of the trust and loyalty of previous generations, they provide us continuity with our past and resources to respond to what shaped that past and might fashion the future, too. Commitment to a particular tradition is not an arbitrary affair, in the sense that some allegedly privileged relationship between tradition and actuality forever eludes verification. No myths or symbols will long retain their power to grasp the consciousness of an individual if they do not really clarify his experience, bring at least a bit of wholeness and integrity to the life of the self, renew faith, and arm people with the hope and love that preparations for tomorrow require.

Faith, hope, and love are not always virtues, of course, even when they appear in Christian dress. As the sources of all our images of the self and perspectives upon the world, they are no less ambiguous and incomplete, no less often twisted and destructive, than are our different points of view. Sometimes it seems as though their main work were the delivery of the self to all sorts of slavery and forms of alienation. Too often the putatively Christian imagination becomes constricted and inflexible, content with the letter instead of committed to the challenges the letter contains, fleeing from judgment and abandoning the lands it was called to explore in order to revive the old idols of some familiar marketplace. From a Christian perspective, however, it is possible to discriminate between diseased and healthy forms of faith, hope, and love.

The disclosure of the one reality that must be approached with ultimate seriousness, the holy source and ground of life, qualifies the seriousness with which we can view ourselves or anything else. The revelation of that which alone is holy accents the irremediable ambiguity of every community, value, or power in the world. Virtue will scarcely be virtuous, then, if it involves no acknowledgment of the difference between God and man that will preclude the confusion of the human with the divine or the divine with the human. It must neither bind us to the world so tightly that we lose ourselves there, nor deflect us from the world so that we are deprived of our own proper possibilities and of our fellowmen. In other words, faith, hope, and love are meant to be *dialectical* phenomena, affirming and denying in the same moment, unities of contraries, committed to *both* this *and* that, conforming to the systole and diastole of the human heart. This dialectic is not enforced upon them in some external fashion by the Christian vision but simply reflects the actuality of ourselves and of the world in which we live. Human nature tells that man is made for God, and so our nature is at war with itself whenever we identify undialectically with what is less than God. Faith, hope, and love are the most common and pervasive ingredients in our life together, as common as hearing or sight, but whenever they lose their dialectical character they begin creating daimons whose power is no less destructive because it is illusory. These three have many forms, but what is most important are not the varieties of love or the versions of faith that men devise, but the difference between bondage and liberty, illness and health.

3
faith, hope, and love

L *ove unites*; it is the venturing of the self beyond itself toward other persons and things, institutions, and values. Only the holy does not need to love, for only the holy is rich and complete in itself. All creatures that populate the earth depend upon others, and love is the power that delivers us to what we require. Man is fashioned in such a way that he cannot live alone; love testifies to this lack of self-sufficiency and provides a token, obscure and twisted, of the relationship to the supremely actual for which man was made. It is natural, then, in the sense that it is a fact before it is a value, fate as well as destiny, necessity as much as choice. There is nothing more to be said uncritically in favor of love than in favor of aggression, which is an equally natural impulse. To be is to love, for love

> is the moving power of life . . . which drives everything that is towards everything else that is. In man's experience of love the nature of life becomes manifest. Love is the drive towards the unity of the separated. . . . The power of love is not something which is added to an otherwise finished process, but life has love in itself as one of its constitutive elements. It is the fulfillment and the triumph of love that it is able to reunite the most radically separated beings, namely individual persons. The individual person is both most separated and the bearer of the most powerful love.[1]

There are different sorts of it, of course, and the Greeks devised several names in order to discriminate among them. Sometimes love is simply a grasping for the elemental necessities of life; sometimes it is an aspiration toward values that transcend our own interests and claim our loyalty despite ourselves. Sometimes, too, love is a gift that we freely offer to others, a response of our strength to their frailty, no longer an expression of our need but of our abundance. Despite these several forms, it still is a drive toward unity. What matters most of all is not whether we choose "higher" instead of "lower" loves, or leave the "physical" for the sake of the "spiritual"—especially because these are the most dangerous—but whether we recognize the threat to ourselves that union inevitably contains.

Love draws the individual not only beyond himself but toward himself, too, for it expresses our appetite for actuality, and there is no actuality as close at hand as the self is to itself. If it does not lure a person to explore the mysteries of his own nature, he will certainly lose his way in his explorations of the world, and all the sooner because the world has devised so many strategies by which to deprive him of himself. Upon the ability to affirm one's own selfhood depend all our powers to affirm other things, for one who cannot affirm his own particular humanity will find no sufficient reason to respect the humanity of someone else. The growth of love into more than selfish appetite and grasping, then, is bound up inseparably with one's own sense of identity, with the recognition that I am who I am and no one else, and that it is not merely an accident but good to be who I am, even though I am not always, and perhaps not very often, a good man.

All of us must acquire some sense of the difference between affirmation of the self and acceptance of what the self does, of course, so that no disgust with what we do will breed contempt for what we are—and so that affirmation of our own singular reality does not become an excuse for doing anything we want. But the indifference and callousness with which we treat others have their source not so much in inordinate love for our own life as in our failure to conserve the sort of taste for the self that can acknowledge the essential fineness of the humanity we all share, as well as recognize the ways that we have savaged it. If we cannot say yes to ourselves we cannot offer ourselves unselfishly to anyone else; we can surrender to them, but we will have lost the gift that we were asked to bring. This sense of the weight and import of our own reality is nothing that we can manage to initiate for ourselves, however; it is a consequence of what others have done to us and for us, and especially within the precincts of the family.

Not only the satisfaction of our love but the tangled roots of our ability to love unselfishly are related to the caring of others—so greatly are we dependent upon what lies beyond ourselves. When love becomes capable of self-denial and sacrifice, it is not only a response to others but the expression of a capacity that depends for its magnitude upon what others first provided for us.

This involution of the movements of the self beyond and toward itself, of unselfish love and self-affirmation, of what the self can offer and what has been offered to the self, reflects twin impulses that reside within the individual—*animus* and *anima*, the active and passive, aggressive and sacrificial, the desire for self-assertion and appetite for self-transcendence. Both are ingredient in our loves, as we seek to gain for ourselves what we find in the world and then surrender ourselves to what we have found. The passion for *ek stasis*, for standing outside and eluding the everyday self through ecstatic union with someone or something else, is a sign now defaced and difficult to read of our ruptured relationship to the holy. As long as God exists, the impulse will remain too violent not to be fulfilled in one fashion or another, and, as long as man is fallen, it is the source of our greatest danger. Constantly luring us beyond ourselves, the thirst for self-transcendence conspires with the world's ambitions to deprive us of ourselves in order to assure its own security, and so there is no justice done to the exigencies of self-affirmation. In the end, therefore, the individual offers nothing to the increase of the realm of the actual, brings nothing to augment the diversity of being. Love becomes a destroyer—not so much because by it I am bound to what is ephemeral and therefore destined to suffer the pain of loss, but for the reason that what is lost is the I.

The biblical story of creation, fall, and reconciliation through Jesus Christ affirms that God does not grudge the creature his own separate realm for the expression of his potentialities and for the increase of his freedom, but offers it to him and calls him to explore its every dimension. As a parable of the meaning of love, the story of *Genesis* tells that love has other aims as well as union, and that when they are forgotten there can be no fulfillment for whatever is loved. The statement that love unites must always be accompanied by a different but equally important claim: *Love separates.* This is the essential dialectic, unity and separation, and when either begins to jeopardize the other, love is diseased.

Love cares more than anything else for the discrete and particular identities of what the self confronts, just as its own finest expressions depend upon the depth of the self's sense of identity; it savors most of all the fascinating and exhilarating fact that this is this and not that. It distinguishes one face from a hundred others, or the smell of a familiar field from the fragrance of alien lands, or the way that arthritis has gnarled these particular fingers from the twist of veins that marks the hand of someone else.

Liberation is the greatest work of love and its ultimate ambition, in the sense that love is intent upon the realization of all the strange and varied potentialities that it has discerned in the one it loves. This is the reason why the act of reconciliation is so important for love, in order that no one should be imprisoned in his own past or in the past of someone else. Sometimes freedom is achieved through the meeting of two selves and sometimes through their parting. Sometimes it is a small affair, a moment when a young boy realizes how good it is to let things go and opens the hand that clutched a tree toad found in the woods on a summer afternoon. But even this private little gesture helps to prepare the boy who will someday become a man for the arduous and aching business of letting another boy go free, despite all the dangers that freedom holds, so that he can be his own creation and not merely a repetition of what his parents were. On the other hand, the reason for rites of passage in every society is simply that the act of liberation is not easy to accomplish, and less so the more deeply we love. Difficult as it is with a child, however, it is no easier in the instance of a wife or husband or friend for us to remember that these are not reflections of myself, that someone else is real.

Because loves emerge from and respond to the mystery of identity, their health depends upon separation as well as union, upon the commitment to distinction as much as the passion for oneness. Indifference cultivates separation and distinction alone, of course, and the only real intent of its sometimes lavish charities is to keep the poor or the different out of sight. But no matter how brutal indifference can sometimes appear, rarely are its consequences so disastrous as what its opposite can effect. Of all debasements of love, the worst are entanglements in which identity is confused and diminished. These do not reflect the absence of love but the loss of love's dialectic, and that is why they so easily lead to hate. Instead of meetings in which each self is enriched by its relationship to another without any violation of its own separateness and integrity, there is a merging in which the individual loses control over his own frontiers. William F. Lynch writes of this sort of invasion of identity, unwitting though it often is, and of the deadly combat it eventually provokes because the self can find no air to breathe:

> The other human being may not be there. He or she may even be dead; but the past and the dead are incorporated into the sufferer, and the desperate battle for one's own feelings and wishes goes on. . . . We know that human feeling and wishing can be transferred to another person, or stolen by another, or lost through a mutual conspiracy with another to the extent that confusion is complete: is this my thought or feeling, or does it belong to another? . . . This is agony, so to melt one's thoughts, wishes, feelings, and self into those of others that one completely loses the taste of self.[2]

The certainty of thoughts and feelings genuinely my own is midwived by the caring of others, but it argues against any sort of symbiotic relationship in which I become nothing but an extension of others who care for me, or of some institution or community beyond myself; it cautions against squandering the self or surrendering its borders just as strongly as it provides the foundation for offering the self to others. In the same way, if love for another self knows what it is about, it will not foster the sort of symbiotic relationship in which I reduce a wife or child or student to an extension of myself and so destroy what first it was that elicited the love. The worst remedy that can be found for uncertainty about one's own identity is the attempt to elevate the self into the center of the life of someone else, so that his or her concern for us provides the assurance of our reality; then both are lost and nothing remains of the second self except a mirror in which the first can glimpse the consequences of its cannibalism. On the other hand, of course, the end is no happier when a person centers his own life upon someone else, living only for this self and inevitably burdening it with a responsibility and a sense of gratitude that are suffocating.

When love seeks union without separation, identity without distinction, the self is dealing with another person or institution or value as though it were not a creature but an absolute. Whenever the finite is mistaken for an absolute, however, what is lost is not only the divine but also everything truly human, because we are violating the way things really are, engaging ourselves in hopeless combat against the actualities of life. This confusion of the human with the divine is the source of daimons that roam our world and whose shadows obstruct our vision. They are born whenever we turn to anything in the world and say, "All I want is you." When we mean what we say, we end with neither you nor I. Sometimes this seems to be the counsel of love, sometimes the dictate of fear, but in robbing a man of himself it sows the seeds of hatred. The daimons are banished only if the strength of love is sapped before hatred can root itself, passion yielding to enervation and obsession to indifference simply because nothing can meet our impossible expectations—except the holy, in its judgment upon them. Then we compensate for our dissatisfaction with actuality by fantasy, and so surrender authentic hope. But the lords of the world continue their insistent clamor that they are all there is, and, despite past treacheries and disappointments, we prepare to listen again and erect more scattered absolutes to obsess and frighten others and ourselves.

The development of modern techniques for the gathering and communication of information can serve as a paradigm of all the factors that conspire to promote the confusion of identity, fostering a vague suspicion that one's thoughts and feelings are not really one's own but have been dictated by an amorphous "they say" whose technological wizardry can homogenize people as easily as milk. Even when the sense of selfhood is not jeopardized by the sickness of love, it is eroded by currents in the everyday world until loving is threatened with the deprivation of what it must possess to be itself. In a mistaken reaction that becomes part of the conspiracy, we race to the rape of our own identity, trying to preserve at least some sense of singularity by the offer of rapid and random confidences before they are invited, by promises to be instantly available to others, to satisfy the idle curiosity of strangers at a moment's notice, to disclose everything anywhere in the hope that a little bit of sensitivity training will go a long way. Even if we are aware of the source and magnitude of our doubts about the reality or worth of the self, we are most often unconscious of the contempt for actuality involved in the failure to recognize that the times of the self have a certain rhythm, a developmental and incremental aspect, movements from lesser to greater and from acquaintance to intimacy, right times for reticence as well as disclosure, for hoarding as well as risk. In our quantified world we simply assume that any moment is as good as the next and that nothing has any special flavor, and so we exile ourselves from knowledge of the deepest meanings of our hope.

Nothing is nobler, nothing is meaner, than the appetite for love and ecstasy. The ambiguity points to the way that all the virtues depend upon one another if any are to find health. Love cannot stand by itself. It is the impulse that shapes both self-affirmation and self-transcendence, but how the exigencies of these equally natural movements can be combined with one another, that is a secret which it does not understand, for there is truth in the old adage that love is blind. It can recognize that it involves separation as well as unity and that whenever one is lost then love itself is dead, but the meaning of its recognition remains obscure. How difficult it is to reconcile the dictates of the two is something that love must ask others to teach. If it is wise enough to acknowledge its own blindness, though, it can hope to learn.

Hope creates; as love draws the self into the realm of the actual, hope begins to discover all the potentiality there and delivers the self to its pursuit. It aspires to the creation of what does not yet exist, the initiation of relationships that the self has not yet sought to achieve, the realization of these possibilities and the rejection of those; and in luring persons to these new adventures it enriches and recreates the people who originally held the hope. Hope drives the self to become more than it was. It is the core of everything that is distinctively human, for man differs from all else in the world because he alone not only has a future but knows there is a future calling to him. Hope unlocks it and carries it back into the present, where it can, often enough, transform and irradiate the whole shape of the day. Hope is creative, then, not only because it counsels the self to actualize more of its own resources but also because it transforms the situation in which the self lives. So it is wrong to regard it as though it were a power that cheats us of the present, diverting our attention from the fragile joys and accustomed responsibilities of the moment toward a promised time that may never come. Because it is love's partner, hope looks for whatever potentiality resides in the actualities of the day. "Hope alone is to be called 'realistic,' " writes Jurgen Moltmann, because it alone takes seriously the possibilities with which all reality is fraught. It does not take things as they happen to stand or lie, but as progressing, moving things with possibilities of change. Only as long as the world and the people in it are in a fragmented and experimental state which is not yet resolved, is there any sense in earthly hopes. The latter anticipate what is possible to reality, historic and moving as it is, and use their influence to decide the processes of history. Thus hopes and anticipations of the future are not a transfiguring glow superimposed upon a darkened existence, but are realistic ways of perceiving the scope of our real possibilities, and as such they set everything in motion and keep it in a state of change.[3]

Love is the movement of life, and hope grasps whatever possibilities that motion holds. The difference between them is that love is natural, needing to be humanized, while hope is human, needing to be tied to the natural. If love does not lead it toward what is actual here and now, the opportunities that it discerns will be nothing except the stuff of dreams and fantasy. Unless it is anchored in the density and detail of our common life, hope will paralyze, not liberate; all its strength and inventiveness are lost when lifted too far above the earth. On the other hand, of course, love needs hope as much as hope depends on love. Love has no tomorrow when hope has fled. There is no reason why men should heed love's counsel and venture into the world except the hope that they will find there whatever they require.

There is a dialectical stance toward the world that hoping involves, similar to and yet different from the involution of self-affirmation and self-transcendence in love. Love reaches for what it can see, and hope reaches despite what it can see. Hope says two things: "not yet" and "despite." It affirms and rejects the world' at the same time, committing itself to the possibilities the present holds but repudiating the constriction of possibilities that the present enforces, refusing to reconcile itself to all that is shabby and coarse and unyielding about today and hoping for something better despite the appearances of things. But when it says no to the ambiguities of today's experience, its denial represents more than nostalgia for a lost paradise, more than wistfulness for we know not what. Hope rejects the world only in the name of the world, only for the sake of what the world might still become. If it ignores the present shape of reality and simply runs away, hope has lost all resources for the creation of anything new.

We often think of hope as a private and internal affair, something that we ought to be ashamed to share with others until some certainty that expectations will not be disappointed renders us invulnerable to ridicule. In fact, however, hope depends upon what lies outside the self not only for its fulfillment but for its particular character; even though community is the source and sustainer of every virtue, hope has a special relationship to it. Despair begins when men are not only aware of their solitude but allow this single fact to grow like a cancer in the life of the mind until the mind can support nothing except the life of this malignancy: I am alone and there is nothing else to say, nothing to do. Captive of an absolute, the self is driven to hopelessness. There is also another form of hopelessness that seems opposed to despair and yet is essentially no different, and this is the presumption that grabs frantically at whatever possibilities it sees, oblivious to other selves and unconcerned for a right time. I am free to do as I wish and condemned to the frenzied pursuit of my wishes because the self is all alone and this moment will never return. It is hopeless to wait for fulfillment at the hands of powers other than our own, and there is no power that can redeem the times. Our presumption of despair and our despairing presumption are equally children of the illusion that community has fallen irremediably and forever apart.

There is one reason why hope can be hopeful, and that is the expectation of help. When its perplexity is very great or its resources obviously unequal to their challenge, the self hopes for help from the earth or perhaps from the holy, sometimes from other selves or simply from the therapy of the passage of time. We are hopeful, however, because not only can we hope *in* others, we can also hope *with* them. We can band together in commitment to some common goal, certainly, but there is an even more internal and important mode of hoping with. I hope for a way out of my present difficulty, but I cannot imagine what it would be and so hope dwindles to ashes. I am a prisoner of my difficulty because the possibilities of my existence do not outstrip my imaginings of it; I cannot intend any sort of action that I cannot imagine myself doing. But if I can put on the imagination of my parents, or of a friend or doctor, or of my wife or sons—or, indeed, if I have at my disposal such a heritage of images that I can respond to the injunction to "have this mind among yourselves, which you have in Christ Jesus (Phil. 2:5)"—then I can gain perspectives I did not have before. From these points of view new possibilities appear and by them old daimons are exorcized. William Lynch sees correctly that:

> Hope not only imagines; it *imagines with.* We are so habituated to conceiving of the imagination as a private act of the human spirit that we now find it almost impossible to conceive of a common act of imagining with. But what happens in despair is that the private imagination, of which we are so enamored, reaches the point of the end of inward resource and must put on the imagination of another if it is to find a way out. This it must do, or it is lost. Despair lies exactly in the constriction of the private imagination. . . . Hope cannot be achieved alone. It must in some way or other be an act of a community, whether the community be a church or a nation or just two people struggling together to produce liberation in each other. People develop hope in each other, hope that they will receive help from each other.[4]

Much as one child asks another to contribute his imaginings to a game in the street, I gain hope by hoping with and through the imaginations of significant others in order to compensate for my own poverty—and in order to defend myself against all the tawdry imagery of mass media that populate consciousness with phantoms and false expectations. Community enables me to realize possibilities that I could never achieve alone, but its even greater service is the enrichment and sobriety of imagination that enables me to grasp possibilities that hitherto I could not begin to see. Therefore, hope continually depends upon the reality of reconciliation, without which I will become a prisoner of my past or of the past of others. We must be ready to forgive one another, else the bonds of community on which hope relies will be frayed beyond service, and then others will bar us from their imaginations and we will not be able to engraft them into our own in a way that augments our possibilities. Hope must have forgiveness instead of recrimination if it is to continue to hope; in this fashion, too, it displays its inseparability from love. The problem, of course, is that there is no escape from our fallenness: imagination is polluted, as much a cesspool as a reservoir, no longer in touch with the expanse and depth of actuality, yours and mine and ours together and the great public one that we never manage to elude. In our imagining together, the difficulties of the self can be compounded instead of remedied. Then, too, there is always the danger of the sort of entanglement in which I do not know any longer whether these feelings are yours or mine, and identity becomes confused.

Nevertheless, the statement that hope creates must still be accompanied by the recognition of something very different: *hope depends.* The essential dialectic of hoping is this involution of creation and dependence. Without the second, the first is impossible; without the first, the second is subhuman. When its two aspects fall out of relation to one another, hope drifts toward fantasy and illusion until it is creative no more, or else we abandon hope, surrender to resignation, and simply give the self away. When it has lost the power to transform self and world, the cause of the failure is the rupture of its partnership with love. Imagination is no longer sufficiently drawn toward the earth to discern actual possibilities, and so the self can do nothing except treat itself as though it were a god, able to reenact the story of *Genesis* and create ex nihilo. The counterfeits of hope seem endless, for fantasy has a million forms. Nevertheless, it is always a covert confession of momentary hopelessness, or at least of helplessness, for its withdrawal from the realm of the actual signals despair either at the powers of the self to transform reality or else at the amenability of some reality to further transformation.

How is it possible to verify whether hope is really hope except in terms of its eventual consequences for the increase of actuality? Has it succeeded in inaugurating a genuine future, involving itself thereby in the futures of others, and so theirs in our own, or has it foreclosed any tomorrow that individuals can begin today to shape and embellish by their own efforts? There is much to be said in behalf of fantasy, of course, for it can be a form of playing that renews a self bruised badly by unremitting commerce with the actual. Sometimes the world is too much for all of us, even the strongest or most faithful; then we must wait, and sometimes there is nothing to do while we wait except perhaps to enjoy the temporary escape that fantasy provides. There are times for fantasies, then, just as there are times for hope. In any event, there is nothing mutually exclusive about the two, and not least among the reasons for that is the pollution of our imagination. They are different points in a spectrum, constantly merging and enveloping one another. But we are lost when we cannot tell one from the other, and, even though it is often difficult to discriminate between them until they have finished their disparate works, there are at least five ways in which they behave very differently—in their attitudes toward hopelessness, waiting, the assistance of others, the present time, and promising.

Genuine hope is well acquainted with hopelessness. It knows that some things simply cannot be hoped for; the world offers no promises to honor every human desire, no matter how self-sacrificial or urgent. I cannot be a child again. I cannot be a man for my son; he must be a man for himself. Hope confronts the hopeless and then tries to outflank it in the search for whatever hope it can realistically entertain. Like fantasy, it contradicts the way things are, hoping for what present facts often will not justify; but in fantasy the real dimensions of the hopeless are not explored, and this evasion is an index of the covert hopelessness that lies in its movement away from actuality. It behaves as though all things were possible, even though the very first lesson taught by the actual is that many things are not possible at all. In other words, it always acts as though it were a god; it is hopeless in its denial of hopelessness just as hope is hopeful because it meets the hopeless and then moves in other directions.

Then, too, hope recognizes that often it must wait for a time when help will come, or when the situation will change or the self will be stronger. Waiting must not be identified with passivity; sometimes it is a courageous and creative act, integral to the achievement of whatever is hoped for, as in the instance of a sick man who awaits the recovery of health. Waiting, indeed, is the most hopeful attitude man can adopt toward the future, and always it is an implicit affirmation that time is the friend no less than the enemy of man. But fantasy is impatient and does not believe there can be value in waiting; it soars far above the constraints of time. It is sudden: everything can be present now and nothing need be not yet. So, of course, it destroys hope, for whatever is not yet is hope's concern.

While hope counts on help not only to achieve what it desires but also for the imagining that sows new seeds of hope, fantasy is invariably a private affair. It can do everything without assistance and likes to hug to itself in the darkness all the implausible dreams and illusions of revenge that it can fashion. Once again the self becomes omnipotent, the rival of God: It can conjure up disaster or delight at will, populating the landscape with a phantasmal army of creatures, benign or threatening, in accordance with its whim. Furthermore, hoping transcends the present only because it first pays attention to whatever is here and now, pressing out its significance and potentiality before hope tries to clothe it in the radiance of the promise of the future. Only after that is hope able to draw next Wednesday night into this afternoon, so that our waiting is invested with significance and threatening facts are relativized by a new temporal context. Fantasy never transforms or expands the shape of the present, though, simply because it forgets to notice it except in the course of a moment of recoil. The escape that it affords may sometimes strengthen the self for tomorrow, but it does nothing to launch the individual into the future in the way that hope can do. Hope comes to the relief of tedium, turning around to scan bits of the present to see if it missed some possibilities when it visited there before. But fantasy surrenders to whatever is boring or seems to be endless; instead of taking arms against it, fantasy simply retreats from the field and leaves the enemy in full command.

Finally, it has nothing to do with promises, while hope is lost without them. They can be the grist of fantasy, of course, but it understands nothing of the actuality of offering and keeping a pledge. We are freed for hope, on the other hand, for no reason except the intricate knot of promises made and implied to ourselves and to others, and received from them, each pledge declaring the advent sometime in the future of a reality that does not yet exist. This interleaving of promises and hopes is what assures me that the future is mine, that I will be part of it as an agent and not only as patient, and that in the midst of its maelstrom of contingencies and necessities there will still be room for fidelity and responsibility to leave their mark. The conjunction of hoping and promising speaks of destiny and not of fate, freedom as well as submission to contingencies we cannot anticipate and powers we cannot hope to match. In its dependence upon others, upon their commitments and their imaginations, hope promises to play fair and hopes for reconciliation if it should betray or be betrayed; it commits itself to be faithful toward its partners, to honor its pledges, to promise that it will not violate the rules of the game and so destroy its grounds for hope. Perhaps this is where it departs most resolutely from the paths of fantasy, which has no commitment to fairness of any sort.

Faith interprets; its trust and loyalty reap for the individual the constellations of symbols and images that invest the ambiguities of his experience with one sort of order or another. At the conclusion of *Cry, the Beloved Country*, there is a chance encounter between Jarvis and Kumalo, whose child is the murderer of Jarvis' only son. The one is a white farmer whose home is in the fertile hills above the poor and drought-stricken village where the other lives, a black priest, but in the mutuality of their loss they have become friends:

> —Do not go before I have thanked you. For the young man, and the milk. And now for the church.
> —I have seen a man, said Jarvis with a kind of grim gaiety, who was in darkness till you found him. If that is what you do, I give it willingly. . . .
> Kumalo said, truly, of all the white men that I have known—
> —I am no saintly man, said Jarvis fiercely.
> —Of that I cannot speak, but God put His hands on you.
> And Jarvis said, That may be, that may be.[5]

Through his dead son and the aged priest, Jarvis has been captured by a new world and it has provided him with a perspective that transcends the exigencies of the moment and its counsels of revenge or despair. It has made him part of a community that spans many generations and provides a bit of remedy, not much but at least something, for his terrible new loneliness. Its common memories provide tales of reconciliation with which he can begin to identify himself, imagery without which there would have been no possibility of friendship with Kumalo or of fidelity toward the ideals of his own son, whom he understands and affirms in death as he never did in life—this is how God put his hands on Jarvis.

Later, the old country pastor contemplates what has been given to him and taken from him during the tragic search for his prodigal son. Wandering in the hills above his village a few hours before his son Absalom is to be executed for the murder that he committed more or less accidentally to gain a few bottles of whiskey and a little money, Stephen Kumalo asks:

> Why was it given to one man to have his pain transmuted into gladness? Why was it given to one man to have such an awareness of God? And might not another, having no such awareness, live with pain that never ended? Why was there a compul-

sion upon him to pray for the restoration of Ndotsheni, and why was there a white man there on the tops, to do in this valley what no other could have done? And why of all men, the father of the man who had been murdered by his son? And might not another feel also a compulsion, and pray night and day without ceasing, for the restoration of some other valley that would never be restored? But his mind would contain it no longer. It was not for man's knowing. He put it from his mind, for it was a secret.[6]

The labyrinthine ways of the holy are more than the mind can contain, and the reasons for everything that happened at Ndotsheni —the new dam and the new church, the new agronomist and the new friendship and the new milk for the children—they are a secret. But the means are clear enough, for the restoration of this valley, and of others like it, depends upon loyalties and images derived from them that will enable vision to discover material from which a strategy of reconciliation can be devised wherever there is brokenness, and to discern signs pointing to other paths that will lead to new and larger hopes wherever hopelessness has blighted familiar fields.

If we are not satisfied with the faiths of Jarvis and Kumalo we will commit ourselves to other ones, for we cannot live without some resources for the clarification of our experience and there is nowhere to turn except to faith. Faith gives love its humanity and hope its realism. It provides the I that loves and hopes, for it is the architect of identity. But it can unman the self, too, if its dialectic is lost. Alone it is sterile, unable to begin its work until informed by the love that will lead it into the realm of the actual and the hope that tempts it to reflect upon what might be but is not yet. On the other hand, faith dictates the directions in which love will turn, for by itself love is blind, while the possibilities that hope will find most worthy of pursuit are decided not by hope itself but from perspectives that are legislated by faith. Love cares for the different identities of the selves and things that populate the earth, and faith for the whys and ways of their interaction. As loyalty and trust, faith sustains the relationships that it has inaugurated; as reliance upon images derived from them in order to interpret us to ourselves as well as to structure our world, it is a consequence and gift of the relationships.

Enough has been written earlier about faith as *fiducia*, in connection with the importance of vision for moral life. In its earliest days, the self learns to trust and then to keep trust in the context of the family, and later by its participation in larger communities. From these relationships, no matter how occasional or frequently ruptured, the individual gathers the mosaic of pictures of himself that gradually enables him to answer the question of his own identity. These images are conveyed in many ways, of course, through political traditions and the fare of the mass media, by the arts, and in the assumptions of our "common faith," but primarily through conversations with all those who are significant others in the life of the self. Sometimes we know them only at a distance, sometimes they are waiting every evening to hear our step at the door, and sometimes our commerce with them grows more intense after they have died than it ever was while they were alive, as in the instance of Jarvis and his son.

Faith must never be mistaken, then, for some complex of emotions or beliefs that the self holds; instead, it is the creator of the self that holds emotions, intentions, or beliefs, although the word also describes the commitments and promises that the autonomous self decides to make. Among the ingredients of these images that our relationships afford are the values to which the self is loyal. We evaluate whatever we see, not least of all when we treat it with indifference, and our standards are written into the grain of our images of the self. They offer the perspective from which we view the world and our own conduct and determine which "facts" will be admitted to consciousness and which ones will be rejected or at least dressed in new clothes. We cannot do without some perspective, and therefore some faith. In the apt words of H. R. Niebuhr:

> It is a curious and inescapable fact about our lives, of which I think we all become aware at some time or another, that we cannot live without a cause, without some object of devotion, some center of worth, something on which we rely for our meaning. In this sense all men have faith because they are men and cannot help themselves.[7]

Whenever faith as *fiducia* asserts its independence of faith as *assensus,* assent to truth, the real nature of the virtue has been entirely misunderstood. If it is one it must be the other, for we can trust only what we know and we try to know better what we trust. Faith is a cognitive affair from the beginning, simply in the sense that it is the foundation of our perspectives; commitments shape cognition and then cognition defines the borders within which we are free to commit ourselves. It is true that faith does not necessarily mean the acceptance of certain propositions, but that is no reason to minimize its cognitive aspect. We can never escape the shadow of our mingled loves and loyalties to find some point of vantage that offers a detached and neutral perspective upon our own relationships, and that is the source of our greatest problem. We will remain prisoners all our lives of the other selves and institutions to which we are related, collaborating with them to assure our own blindness, if the statement that faith interprets is not balanced by a very different claim: *faith doubts.* The essential dialectic of faith is the involution of interpretation and doubt; when either fails, the other also is vitiated. Nothing remains for the task of interpretation when questioning ends, of course, and doubt is meaningless apart from a context of interpretation that renders its questions significant.

This is not simply to say that faith is assailed by doubts about the truth of what it believes, although that occurs frequently enough. Nor does it point only to the humanness of the imagery that faith employs or to the modest validity of all language devised for the interpretation of the human when it is used in order to speak of our relationship to the holy. Tillich correctly emphasizes what must be true of every sort of faith that has not succumbed to serious disease, no matter whether directed toward the holy or to some reality no more than human:

> If faith is understood as belief that something is true, doubt is incompatible with the act of faith. If faith is understood as being ultimately concerned, doubt is a necessary element in it. It is a consequence of the risk of faith. . . . It does not question whether a special proposition is true or false. It does not reject every concrete truth, but it is aware of the element of insecurity in every existential truth. At the same time, the doubt which is implied in faith accepts this insecurity and takes it into itself in an act of courage. Faith includes courage. Therefore, it can include the doubt about itself.[8]

The doubt that Tillich mentions has to do with the concrete and contingent element in faith, its constellation of symbols and the uncertainty of existential truth. What requires the greatest doubt, however, is not the symbolism we use but *why* we see and trust as we do, not the substance of vision but the perspectives we employ.

We live in nets, all of us, webs of illusion that we have spun from ourselves and our relationships, and there is no escape if we do not learn to question our questions as well as the answers they find. If we do less, the faiths from which we gain our identity will eventually deprive us of their gift. Faith brings us the resources to develop a way of seeing so that we can put questions to the world, but it will blind us if it does not involve the acknowledgment that it is man himself who is questioned and his way of seeing that is most questionable of all. On the one hand, there is the inexpugnable selfishness of our perspective, in the sense that the shadow of the self falls all across its own vision, darkening the landscape until we can find no way to see what really is there. On the other, there are all the different perspectives offered by our various relationships, united only by their selfishness. We hope for reconciliation, for a perspective on perspectives, but each candidate seems to exclude something valid that another represents.

The heart of the matter, though, is the anomaly that our perspectives are not our own even though each of them is indisputably tainted by a selfishness that very much is ours. Our questions are not really devised by ourselves but are legislated for us by the relationships in which we stand. When we stop questioning our questions, then, we have tacitly accepted as absolutes the other selves and communities and institutions to which we are related and from which we derive the perspectives that decide what questions we shall ask. This confusion of the human with the divine is much more than a minor instance of mistaken identity, more than a momentary error that will do the self no damage. Instead, it destroys the individual, robbing him of any independence and integrity of his own. Vision and judgment are surrendered to the principalities and powers of the world by the workings of the same faith that originally awarded them to the individual. We are alienated in the most profound sense of being "nothing but" these larger realities. If we try to elude the daimons we have made by adopting a more or less cynical relativism that regards every perspective as equally valid, and therefore equally worthless, we fall into a form of bondage as terrible as any other, victim of casual appetites and pawn of whatever occurs in the everyday world.

There are special Christian reasons to insist upon the inseparability of interpretation and doubt. Man is radically accountable
and entirely questionable, simply because he stands before God.
In other words, the self is judged not only for what it thinks and
does but for the creation of a self that thinks and acts in these
ways, not only for the motives on which it acts but for the construction of a self that will act on such motives, not only for how
it responds to what it sees but for the fashioning of a way of seeing that grasps these things and fails to notice those. The adoption
of every more expansive loyalty and every greater image of the
possibilities or obligations of selfhood involves an acknowledgment of responsibility for what the self is, and a recognition that
the I who acknowledges therefore transcends every imaginative
grasp of his own selfhood.[9] The nature of the self, then, is no
longer the context within which man is responsible, but has itself
become the responsibility of a creature with endless possibilities
of self-transcendence. Christian faith counsels men that they are
always unfinished, more than they can begin to envision until they
possess new ways of seeing that will relativize and expand the
familiar ones.

We are responsible before God not only for the consequences
of our vision but for the perspective itself. Not only is it as questionable as everything else but it is even more urgently in need of
constant questioning, for it is the source of everything else. Doubt,
therefore, is concerned with the roots of the affair, not with the
validity of interpretation but with its presupposition. Reconciliation and renewal in Jesus Christ can render a man more sensitive
to the dangers that all perspectives involve, but they do not enable
him to adopt some marvelous new point of vantage untainted by
the self; after all, it is I who see. It can never be otherwise; the
images that fashion our perspectives reflect where we stand and
afford no more than very human points of view, bound up with
earthly loves and loyalties. That is the reason why the figure of
the self as player and the image of the good life as fair play—
implicates as they are of the disclosure of a reality that must be
approached with ultimate seriousness—are particularly important.
They warn us against forgetting how questionable our vision always remains.

If our fallenness is sometimes disclosed by our faithlessness,
its magnitude is far more evident in our excessive faith in faith

and in the lapse of doubt. When interpretation and doubt come unstitched, faith no longer acknowledges the lordship of God or else it betrays the self into servitude to lords of the world and powers of the everyday that deprive it of any independence of its own. If it loses its essential dialectic, in other words, it suffers the same disease that infects love and transforms its object into a *daimon* or that pollutes hope and drives it to despair. One presence or incident is made an absolute, and now this single reality dominates vision and obscures everything else, blinding us to its real relationships with other things. Sometimes it is a power outside man, sometimes a dream within. They are no different, though, for illusions hold awesome power, and powers regarded as ultimate are invested with all sorts of illusory properties. Man loses his freedom, and either he learns to hate what torments him or else he becomes contemptuous of his own reality, for in one way or another it cannot meet the demands of the adversary that it has itself created. Whenever the earthly and human are confused with the divine, the human disappears.

There are remedies for hatred and despair, of course, if only we can see what they are. But there are none for the absolutism of the assumption that one's own values constitute the standard of all that is valuable, that one's own perspective is beyond dispute, that it is author of questions but subject to none, established and assured by powers and institutions secure from any challenge. If we fall into that illusion, we will never be able to see beyond the range of our disease. So what begins as faith and loyalty and then develops complex patterns of interpretation must finish in silence and waiting, questioning everything it has done, doubting most of all the premises with which it worked. There are always some certainties but, as Kumalo understands, much is "not for man's knowing." There is no need to question, for example, whether the dawn will come, "as it has come for a thousand centuries, never failing. But when that dawn will come, of our emancipation, from the fear of bondage and the bondage of fear, why, that is a secret."[10]

Love, hope, faith—the impulse toward whatever is actual within the self and beyond it, the aspiration toward whatever is possible and for the time to achieve it, the interpretation that orders the realm of the actual and unveils its real possibilities. Without these three, no life, no wholeness for the self, nothing for the self at all and the self is nothing. Love is a response to the identities of selves and things; it always depends upon others and first of all upon the others who assured the child that it was quite all right to be human and to be a child and to be this particular and thoroughly remarkable one. Then hope, in order to hope, accepts the imaginations of others and offers its own to them, envisioning their help and the help of the earth. Faith deepens the sense that humanity is a gift from others, for the images it involves are derived from the relationships of the self to other persons and communities. If faith becomes Christian, then all the imagery of this tradition reinforces the conviction that selfhood means being for and being with others and that man fulfills himself in giving. Faith, hope, love: all attest that existence means responsiveness and mutuality, being with one's own self and with others and with the earth—and sometimes, or for some, in and through these different relationships being also with God.

Healthy love means the triumph of integrity against all the tendencies, internal and external, to invade others or to suffer their invasions of the self and so fall into the everydayness in which one no longer lives but is lived through by someone or something else. At its best, faith means the triumph of integrative vision against all the temptations to become obsessed with isolated facts until they fill the whole window of the mind. Real hope means the triumph of inventiveness and freedom against whatever threatens to reduce the self to a patient or frighten it away from the possibilities that reside in the realm of the actual. Each of the virtues has its own distinct identity and yet each one, like man himself, depends upon others if it is to be victorious in the constant warfare of integrity against invasion, integrative vision against the tyranny of an absolute, the integration of today and tomorrow against captivity to the present or past. Integrity, the integrative, integration—the meaning of salvation is wholeness, the restoration of health and the recovery of unity. Salvation means the integration of realities that first seem opposed, like unity and separation, creativeness and dependence, interpretation and doubt, but that disclose in the end not only their connections but their complete dependence upon one another.

Faith, hope, and love have a thousand forms, for nothing is commoner than they; in some of them our humanity finds its finest expressions, while in others we wound ourselves and torment our neighbors. Consequently, within the Christian tradition it has sometimes been a convention to discriminate between common and saving forms of the virtues. The distinction is intended to pay some theological honor to those elements in ordinary life that are necessary for the construction of identity while strictly differentiating between Christian or "supernatural" virtues and these lesser brethren. But the procedure is unsatisfactory and should be abandoned; the clarity it is alleged to achieve is purchased at the cost of tremendous distortion. The reasons that militate against the distinction are the same ones, of course, that expose the inadequacy of the notion of "theological virtue." On the one hand, it obscures the natural roots of Christian life and the social character of our experience, for there are continuities between the humblest and most exalted forms of faith, hope, and love. The ways that we are loved and trusted and liberated by parents and peers provide important keys for deciphering the meaning of Christian claims. Then, too, familial love often seems to contain an impulse not only to turn inward but to direct itself toward the whole family of man. The discontinuities may be far greater and more important than the continuities, but still H. R. Niebuhr is persuasive when he argues against any view of the Christian forms of faith, hope, and love that interprets them as supranatural additions to nature:

> The love of God and of the neighbor in God are not foreign to man's nature . . . but in our fallen situation they are present as love of idol and love of the neighbor in relation to idols. Man does not exist without love of an objective good which is, in a momentary way, at least the object of his greatest concern. . . . Similarly, man being not merely gregarious but personally communal does not live without relations of fidelity and trust, though in a world of many betrayals, trust turns partly into mistrust, and loyalty to partial causes leads to betrayal of other causes. Trust and faithfulness together with the secondary form of faith, belief, are inseparable from man's existence as a communal, personal being who must make promises in order to be a person and must trust in promises. But the structure of faith is warped, twisted and perverted in actual existence and must be both restored and perfected.[11]

On the other hand, saving forms of the virtues are not as pure as they seem, and nowhere is their lack of purity quite so evident as in their pretensions to have it. Lesser and greater faiths, loves, and hopes constantly interpenetrate one another, for better and for worse and certainly far beyond our understanding. The chief difficulty with the distinction, though, is somewhat different from the problems that surround the idea of "theological virtue." At least from a Christian perspective, when the varieties of faith, hope, and love that inform our common life lose their dialectical character, the consequence is that they gain a new dimension that is obdurately theological. Precisely because we are fallen but not fallen so far that we can obliterate the passion for the divine that is part of our essential nature, all our versions of the virtues tend to inhabit a sort of theological continuum. The attempt to discriminate among some forms that are saving and others that are common, then, seems consonant neither with the actualities of the situation nor with Christian criticism of it.

When the impulse toward union and the need for separation clash with one another in our loves, they breed daimons that populate a darkly theological landscape, and we are held in bondage there. When interpretation and doubt dissolve their proper marriage in the act of faith, we invest with ultimacy the selves and powers from which our perspectives are derived, and so we betray ourselves into the hands of the daimons again. When we fail to see the inseparability of dependence and creativity, the self lives with the sterile supposition that it can be its own god or else it surrenders to some of the gods that inhabit the earth. In our loving, in our hoping, in our keeping and breaking of faith, scattered absolutes are born that witness despite themselves to a human hunger that nothing human satisfies. Only indifference or enervation will keep them at bay, but the hunger is in us still. We are prey to a sort of wistfulness, then, an appetite for glory beyond anything the eye can see. Even the fulfillment of hope creates a little abscess of disappointment in the consciousness of the self, just as there is a certain sad ambiguity about the fulfillment of love because it threatens the separation that fires love and on which life depends. At the root of our dissatisfaction there is a passion for the divine that can assume many weird and twisted forms but that cannot be extinguished because it is the correlate of the reality of God as the source and end of human life. By displaying the theological continuum into which all sorts of common forms of faith and hope and love are thrust because of the loss of their essential dialectical character, theological ethics can perform one of the fundamental tasks of natural theology and offer some modest support for a Christian anthropology.

Hope can hope for many things, but it cannot hope to escape a theological dimension within itself unless its strength is lost, not because of any answers it discerns but by reason of the implications of its questions. Moltmann writes:

> Man's hopes and longings and desires, once awakened by specific promises, stretch further than any fulfilment that can be conceived or experienced. However limited the promises may be, once we have caught in them a whiff of the future, we remain restless and urgent, seeking and searching beyond all experiences of fulfilment, and the latter leave us an aftertaste of sadness. The "not yet" of expectation surpasses every fulfilment that is already taking place now.[12]

The selves and powers on which hope depends betray it all too frequently, but there is something paradoxical about the consequences, for even these betrayals kindle new hopes that hope not only for fidelity instead of faithlessness but for more than the greatest faithfulness could provide. Our possibilities and our desirings grow strangely less commensurate as more of the possibilities we desired are realized. We ask not simply for more of what we have but for something different and better, and yet we do not understand what the aspiration means or whom it seeks. The lessons of experience counsel very modest expectations, while from somewhere we still garner shapeless hopes that are maintained despite our certainty that the world will not honor them. And in all this there is the suspicion that we have not simply deluded ourselves, that there is some source beside or beyond illusion from which these yearnings come.

The real distinction to which the idea of virtue leads, therefore, is not the difference between natural and theological or between common and saving; it is the tension between sickness and health. On the one hand, not only the demands of life before God that discipleship alone acknowledges but also the actualities of our common life that everyone encounters call for a dialectical stance toward the self and its world. To find this is health. On the other, there is the temptation of a false simplicity that will have nothing to do with ambiguities or with the unity of contraries and that will usher us into a world much more than human and therefore also much less. To fall into this is sickness. Whenever we manage to recover the dialectic that existence requires, the virtues become the guardians of what is finest in our humanness. Whenever we do not, they are our destroyers. Their health depends upon the vitality of the imagination, though, and it is not easy to keep watch on the imagination. When it becomes ill or grows impoverished, the virtues wither and there is nothing to do except wait in the hope that the images of hope will come again. But if hope is to prove creative, it is important that we should not ignore the mislocation of the problem of human existence that the idea of virtue has sometimes seemed to suggest.

PART TWO

4

dialectics
and daimons

In the everyday world we do not manage to maintain with any consistency the essential dialectics of faith, hope, and love. Their disintegration in the midst of the ambiguities of experience does not mean that doubt swallows interpretation, however, or that dependence renders all creativeness impossible. On the contrary, it is the dialectic that is lost, not the realities that it relates to one another, although the consequences for them are various and severe. What the disruption means is that the strength of one element is no longer proportional to the vitality of the other; no longer is it true that as one grows more intense the other is enriched as well. In a relationship with someone else who addresses me as "thou," for example, the other self suddenly fills my whole world and in that moment there is nothing else I see. The intensity of the relationship contributes to my own sense of manhood; it firms my grip upon my own integrity. I become more genuinely myself than ever I was before the word of this "thou" who, in becoming all my world, offers me a world that is truly my own. The moment of address has unlocked new dimensions within myself, and I run the fingers of my mind through riches of the self that are indisputably my own and yet that I could never summon when I was alone. The other self is not an absolute that bars me from the world but a person who renders it human for me and me more human in it.

As the dialectic weakens, our common experience is that the strength of one element seems to damage the life of the other, and so unity blurs our sense of separateness or dependence inhibits creativity. But the partners that have fallen apart can also wound one another in such fashion that the stronger discovers that its victory has somehow gutted its own powers, and now it is subverted by the misdirection of whatever energy remains in the weaker. For example, the primary object of our doubting now becomes the substance of our vision instead of the perspective from which we see. This subversive doubt is a reaction that our interpretive venture itself fosters, because the consequences of its undisciplined vitality are prejudice and ideology, kindling new doubts by inciting different prejudices and conflicting ideologies to compensate for what it now fails to see. Without a taste for the pervasive ambiguities of life, either we impose our perspectives upon the world without acknowledging their relativity or else we abandon perspective and surrender to factuality too soon, before imagining and interpretation have worked their magic on it. We fail to recognize how drastically our questioning of reality throws our own selves into question, or else we question too much our own intimations and most elemental hungers because of the walls of "brute fact" that surround us. We doubt ourselves too much or not enough. In the one we credit ourselves with less than humanness and in the other with more, but in either the human is gone.

In our hoping, too, we come to depend upon other selves and powers, not simply for provision of the resources that are necessary for our own creativeness but so that we need not face the burden of creation. We run away from our own reality and expect others to compensate for whatever we do not want to perform for ourselves. We do not appropriate for ourselves their imaginations, bathing them in the special light of our own perspectives, but simply hide there from the weaknesses that we find in ourselves. This sort of dependence is the enemy of creativity, of course, but sometimes the source of its misdirection is the false assumption with which creativity begins. We persuade ourselves that we ought to be able to accomplish anything to which we set our hand and that dependence is a sign of immaturity; we mean to be like gods. But we discover many things that the self cannot begin to do and then the illusion avenges itself upon us. Cheated by impossible expectations, we fall back into immature dependence, and creativity falters because it was not content with the modest but real nourishment provided by dependence of a different kind. In our confusion there is an inchoate suspicion that we have duped ourselves; a willful element is working in our blindness, and it tugs intrusively at the corners of consciousness.

In the same fashion we love too little or too much, not wisely but too well, and if we love too much we find that the vigor of one passion vitiates another and so it is still true that we love too little, too. We withhold too much in order to safeguard ourselves, and passion fades to a mild habit, without risk and equally without reward in the hours of tedium and diminished appetite when nothing seems able to call us beyond our routinized ways. Or we offer too much and lose the self that offered, losing even real unity because now the self is gone. But it is difficult to resist the thirst for ecstasy that torments us, beckoning the individual toward the *ek stasis* of death if it can discover nothing within the realm of the actual that is able to rapture the self beyond itself. We follow the paths to which the exigencies of self-affirmation point and discover they lead to the same larger selves of communities and institutions to which we are called by our appetites for self-transcendence. There we learn again that he who finds his life will lose it; somehow we have misdirected ourselves or have been misdirected; we have misunderstood the signs along the way or failed to notice an important turn.

So the humanization of the resources within the self that the idea of virtue describes seems more a dream than a proper hope. Our desires are immoderate, somehow fallen away from any correlation with the satisfactions that actuality can provide, or else we lose our appetite for satisfaction. Perspective is gone and so sometimes we grasp for too much, sometimes for too little; desire gnaws at us too sharply, or else we cannot fan its embers to flame again at all. The inevitable penalty of man's separation from the supremely actual is that his desires should lose their relationship to the satisfactions that actuality can provide. Nor is "reason" a trustworthy ally in the process of humanization, and not only because the self constantly gets in its own way and then cannot see beyond itself. Man's estrangement from the holy corrupts the core of his selfhood. The victory of reason over all the currents that eddy within us, therefore, remains part of the problem and not a solution. How we reason depends upon where we stand to view the world; our point of vantage is derived from our images of ourselves, and these are given to us by our covert faiths as well as by the ones that we confess. Even the best is marred by selfishness. So man will not save himself by reason, and indeed, if crimes committed by the self against itself in the name of reason were tried in a court of law, none of us would ever escape from jail.

The problem with reason is that it cannot discern, much less universalize, the integral relation between giving and receiving, sacrifice and fulfillment, constraints and freedom, self-affirmation and self-transcendence. The cause of its incapacity is simply that it cannot find a context within which these relationships make any consistent sense at all. Their justification requires a faith that extends the assumption of "basic trust" beyond our small communities, precisely because the divine will have been there before us. The world as we see it is a selfish place, however, ruled by contingencies, breeding uncertainties, disrupted by accidents, characterized by boredom and suddenness; whatever imagination might dictate on the assumption of basic trust has little rationality in a realm where promises are few and even these are broken as often as kept. The world offers little to support the claim that he who loses his life will find it again.

Basic trust, of course, does not counsel that the self is either invincible or invulnerable. It describes a taste for the self and a sense of its worth that enable an individual freely to exercise his agency, confident that his context is amenable to change by human activity and willing to act on the assumption that the selves and powers to which he is related will deal fairly with his own best interests, often enough despite his misunderstandings of what those interests really are. Despite all that is random and brutal about the world, its intentions toward man must be assumed to be ultimately not less than fair; so for those who have eyes to see them, there are connections between new constraints and greater freedoms, present judgment and future opportunity.

But what does it mean to write of treatment that is ultimately not less than fair? The truth as we know it is that we deal unfairly with others and are ourselves the sometime victims of gross unfairness, gratuitous suffering, and undeserved tragedy. Basic trust means no superficial hopefulness in the face of this but a determination to confront suffering and death and learn what they have to teach, not to pretend that they do not exist and so gain nothing in recompense for their robberies and the violence they practice. In other words, basic trust affirms that vision will be fairly rewarded and that nothing is unworthy of attempts to encompass it within the range of our sight. This is much more, as well as much less, than a shallow optimism that never confronts the harsh and daimonic realities of human life. It counsels that the single path to wisdom, to the remarkable illuminations that render small lives memorable, is the way that leads into the depth and detail of common life. If we look elsewhere for insight and take what promises to be a shorter road, we are no longer persons of basic trust, our road will dwindle to ruts we cannot negotiate, and we will lose our way in the night. It is certainly true that the possibilities of the self as moral agent will be curtailed if the individual cannot maintain the assumption of basic trust. But there are even better reasons for its maintenance, and the best of them, except for the presence of God, is the knowledge that more strength and more creativeness have been elicited from us on dark days than in happier times. We do not win every battle, but at least there is a chance to learn from them all.

Basic trust, therefore, is diametrically opposed to the absolutizing instinct that sees no connections anywhere and that populates its universe with hordes of little "nominalist particulars." Then the self finally becomes the victim of obsession with one of them that excludes all the others and blocks a person from commerce with the real world, chaining him to its own isolated particularity and to nothing else at all. Even the possibility of basic trust is foreclosed if the dialectic in our loves and faiths and hopings grows so weak that we begin to create scattered absolutes that preoccupy and frighten people. The two are inextricably entangled: unless the dialectic is restored the adult has no power to recover the basic trust that others inspired in him so easily when he was a child, but without the basic trust there is no foundation on which to attempt the rebuilding of the dialectic.

Hope seems to introduce us to the root of the problem, to the source of reason's incapacity to discern what basic trust involves, because it is first to recognize the threats that live in the future. Our many faiths, perhaps just in the stubbornness with which we cling to the imagery they provide, always tell of our anxiety before the future and form part of the mistaken quests for security or anodynes that anxiety inspires, and some of these quests are resident in every version of Christian faith. A cloudless day is shadowed by anxieties that, for no good reason, tarnish the simplest and most innocent of pleasures. Caught in the welter of memories of last night's dreams, we stop a game played by children on a quite safe street and reduce them to victims of the strange traffic of our adult apprehensions. Our unreflective illusions of immortality are suddenly displaced by the imagined symptoms of perhaps incurable disease, and the displacement argues the presence of still a different sickness. Clutching to life without particular regard for the quality of life, we recoil from the drive toward death within ourselves, checking our rush into the future because of the sudden fear that it seeks the end and not a new beginning. The future is cause for anxiety, of course, for it is unknown, and all we know is how insecure and vulnerable our present arrangements are. It is all the more threatening because we know no sovereign power that can place the future at our disposal, except the power of accident and the misrule of chance.

So we turn our backs toward tomorrow and wait for it to transform itself into the impotent past, forgetful of the power that the past wields in the future, or else we work with unremitting seriousness to assure our own sovereignty and survival, building all sorts of fortified cities that we hope accidents cannot invade. Then, of course, we still turn our backs toward tomorrow, scurrying around in the past and present to arm ourselves against whatever lies ahead instead of preparing ourselves to make it our own. Because man is the one creature who not only possesses a future but knows that he possesses it, he is also the one creature who can deliberately foreclose his own futurity, and so he does, only to return to it again because the past is a history of promises broken and in the present everything has gone flat and stale.

In the ways that it exiles itself from a genuine tomorrow, however, the self seems no more than a minor accomplice of powers greater than itself; the social character of our experience forces a measure of alienation upon us even before we are betrayed by the passion for ultimacy engraved in our nature. The dialectical nature of the virtues is lost not only because of the disordering within ourselves, not only because of the weight of our selfishness and the deficiencies of our perspectives, but even more because of the pretensions of the powers that structure the world in which we live. Every community and institution counsels us to understand ourselves in terms of nothing but certain roles and functions that it affords, and to find our surest defense and greatest comfort precisely in this "nothing but." These powers and principalities assure us that they are anchored in "the nature of things" and therefore can satisfy the appetite for ecstasy that is intensified by our anxiety in the face of the future. We evade the recognition that we too have had a hand in the production and maintenance of our social world, that we are the ones who utter these claims as well as respond to them, and so we identify ourselves entirely with the roles that the world offers. It is never slow to accept the gift of ourselves, for otherwise it would betray its pretensions to represent the nature of things and to be able to resolve the question of our relationship to the "really real." As Jean-Paul Sartre comments, then:

> There is the dance of the grocer, of the tailor, of the auction-eer, by which they endeavor to persuade their clientele that they are nothing but a grocer, an auctioneer, a tailor. A grocer who dreams is offensive to the buyer, because such a grocer is not wholly a grocer. Society demands that he limit himself to his function as a grocer, just as the soldier at attention makes himself into a soldier-thing with a direct regard which does not see at all, which is no longer meant to see. . . . There are indeed many pre-cautions to imprison a man in what he is, as if we lived in per-petual fear that he might escape from it, that he might break away and suddenly elude his condition.[1]

The persuasiveness of what the world tells us is all the greater because of the inescapable limitations involved in our encounters with ourselves. There is a secret citadel of selfhood, something more to the "I" that is acknowledged whenever we accept respon-sibility for what we have made of ourselves until now. But it is never approached in abstraction from what we have made of our-selves and have been made by others in our everyday lives; I cannot be with myself in isolation from what I am in the world and from the ways in which I know myself perceived. More than functions and roles I may be, but apart from them the "I" dis-solves and I can no longer encounter my own self. Alienation is not only a fate visited upon the self by the constraints of the everyday world, then, nor simply a way of life that the individual hastens to embrace in order to ease the burdens and uncertainties of a future that will be someday, as the reality of death bears mute testimony, more than a match for him. It is also a consequence of our inability ever to see ourselves in abstraction from the roles and chores of the everyday world. We have few options in the end, and alienation seems no poor choice, for we can fulfill our roles and duties with some decency and honor, and, after all, these things are not unimportant.

No one can escape a measure of alienation; in certain times and places, at least, we are "nothing but," wholly defined by our relationships to family or nation, caste, and class. Then the thirst for some version of ecstasy beyond the ones we derive from our unity with these communities and powers grows far less exigent, for our "nothing but," whatever it is, assures us of a perspective that is absolute as long as it endures. We are salvaged from anomie; we are no longer called into question; we need not fear the dictates of "they say" because, of course, now we are they. There are many reasons why the dialectic of our loving and hoping and trusting is lost: the pretensions of the social world to represent the nature of things, the limitations in our encounters with ourselves, the ambiguities of present experience and the threat of the future, our enervation as well as our passion for ultimacy, and behind all of them the rupture of our relationship with God. Whatever the reason, though, the consequence is always the same.

Man is never left alone, or at least he will not leave himself alone, although there is scant reason for comfort in that. The final surrender of the self for which our nature trembles can justify itself only by investing with ultimacy some earthly power. If enervation or indifference blunts our impulse toward self-transcendence, instead of creating new absolutes we capitulate to the everyday and find in its quiet tyranny still another absolute. We are not long content simply to meet the populace of the earth; it is far easier to repopulate the world with our own creations than to acknowledge that someone else is real. We fashion for ourselves a new reality that serves as a surrogate for the holy presence we can no longer find, and it is the reality of the daimonic; this is our own fabrication, but the artificer becomes its captive. The daimonic is born whenever men try to identify the divine with the human and so deprive themselves of what the human really holds.

Daimon means genius; it is the power that elevates an individual beyond the routine actualization of his capacities, an enrichment and enchantment of imagination that enables a person to become far more than he has been hitherto. On the other hand, *daimon* also denotes an inferior divinity, a power that is not divine at all in the sense that it is particularly attached to a certain place or to a single individual and cannot venture beyond the small precinct where it rules. It becomes a power for evil instead of good simply because it cannot leave its own temple; it is the patron of the singular and individual entity which is divested of relationships to anything beyond itself, not relativized by its context and placed in perspective. Daimons are the guardians of "nominalist particulars," small absolutes that bar men from access to the expanse and depth of the realm of the actual. Daimons are the children of faith, of course; so, too, are they always bent on patricide, seeking an end to the interpretive venture. No matter what is absolutized, whether it is some closed society or a certain constellation of values, the conventions of the everyday or the will of the manipulative individual, the sovereignties that men fashion over themselves are daimons that disclose their true nature because they confine the individual to a particular place where he cannot see the dimension of depth within himself and in others, and it is this dimension alone through which the holy is known.

How deeply etched the passion to locate the divine in the human can be, so that its disappointment transforms the beloved into an object of hate, even if it is one's own self rather than someone else, is the story that François Mauriac tells in *Vipers' Tangle*. Louis is an old lawyer who has spent half a century in the implacable pursuit of wealth and power, or so he believes until he realizes that he is spending his last days in a search for some way to disinherit his family. When he recognizes that hatred has managed to put all desire to flight, he also understands that it has been the strongest passion in himself for many years and that he has never really served the gods to which he protested his devotion.

> After all, what had I been doing, for years, except trying to get rid of that fortune, load it upon somebody who was not of my own family? I have always been mistaken about the object of my desires. We do not know what we desire. We do not love what we think we love. . . . I have been a prisoner all my life long to a passion which did not possess me. As a dog barks at the moon, so I was fascinated by a reflection.[2]

The figure of the monster or *daimon* appears throughout the story and carries us to the heart of the matter. Louis often uses the image to describe himself and his "old, surly, terrifying face, that Medusa's head,"[3] as well as to characterize the whole pack of his children and grandchildren. Shortly before his death he comments wearily that nothing in him, not even his gestures or laugh, does not belong to the monster to whom he gave his name. The confession falls appropriately in the context of his recognition of the involution of crime and punishment. His crime had not lain in avarice, or even in hatred, but in the warped vision that had provided a place where hatred could take root. Then hatred had reinforced his blindness, of course, depriving him of any possibility to see all that was there in the world beyond the self or to recognize what was not there at all, and so

> to seek beyond those entangled vipers. . . .
> It had not been enough for me, throughout half a century, to recognize nothing in myself except that which was not I. I had done the same thing in the case of other people. . . . Never had the appearance of other people presented itself to me as something that must be broken through, something that must be penetrated, before one could reach them.[4]

The roots of his alienation, the seeds from which he grew into a monster in a monstrous land where there were surfaces but never depths, where everything seemed more or less than human, lay in his childhood imaginings of himself as a boy whom no one could love. He had believed himself one of "those whose presence spoils everything," and he acted in accordance with this illusory image that really imputed more than human powers to himself, and so "youth was nothing but one long suicide. I hastened to displease on purpose for fear of displeasing naturally."[5] It seemed, indeed, quite "unimaginable" when an attractive girl named Isa fell in love with him, and all the more so because her family was even wealthier and more prestigious than his own. "I had ceased to repel, I was not hateful," Louis later writes to his wife. "What counted was my faith in the love which you had for me. I saw my reflection in another human being; and my image, thus reflected, had nothing repulsive about it."[6] Accepted by another person, he finally comes to affirm and cherish the humanity within himself. One night in bed, however, not long after their marriage, Isa rather idly tells her husband the story of an earlier engagement that was broken when the boy and his parents learned there was a history of serious illness in her family.

She tells Louis not to be jealous and he quickly agrees, for "how could you have understood that the tragedy was played out beyond all jealousy?"[7] The truth, as he is determined to understand it because of all the confirmation his old image of himself provides, is that Isa and her family had "swooped hungrily upon the first snail" they saw.[8] That is a lie, and even Louis is not unaware of the element of self-deception that feeds his anguish, but still it compels him to become the self of his childhood dreams, betrayed by disappointment and willful blindness into old habits of imagination that convince him "it was all a sham. She lied to me. I am not set free. How could I have thought that any girl would fall in love with me? I am a man whom nobody can love."[9] From that night on he contents himself with a series of brief affairs, scarcely concerned to conceal them even from his wife, setting out deliberately to treat other selves as nothing more than objects because of the illusion that he has been used in the same way. The memory of what Isa told him eats away his consciousness of everything else, a bloated presence that occupies the whole range of the old man's vision.

So the relationship between Louis and his wife does not end in some sort of conjugal truce but sours to hatred, hatred for himself as well as for her, precisely because of the magnitude of his thirst for a disinterested or gratuitous love. The frustration of this yearning for a love that will plunge straight to the elusive self hidden beneath all its deeds and appearances has terrible consequences, for it blinds Louis to everything about himself that lies beneath the planes and angles of his Medusa's head, as well as to the humanity of Isa, and renders quite impossible any form of love at all. As always, it is passion for something more than human that reduces the human to less than itself, and yet that passion lies at the core of our humanness and is what distinguishes us from the other creatures that inhabit the earth. The mode of Louis' revenge reduces him to a slave of objects that can offer no compensation for the inevitable failure that occurs whenever a person tries to force the ambiguities of the human to yield something that the holy can provide, but the holy alone.

The conclusion of *Vipers' Tangle* suggests that Louis has come to accept the truth of Christianity before he dies. But the evidence lies not so much in any explicit declaration as it does in the humanizing of expectations that the old lawyer finally achieves. A new attitude toward his family informs a compassionate reflection of which he would have been incapable in earlier times: "who knows whether they are not prisoners, as I was myself, of a passion which does not belong to the part of their nature that is deepest."[10] The days before his death are spent in attempts to comfort a granddaughter whose marriage has disintegrated. Louis has been converted to the human, and, even though so many years have been wasted and so little time remains, this is still a gift of God. The humanizing of the man is itself persuasive testimony that the holy has drawn close, for the revelation of God means the humanizing of what one expects from the self and from other people; it exacts a commitment to ask for no more than the human can provide, as well as to content oneself with nothing less.

If there is no word from beyond the human situation, then, man tends to search for too much in man, and, because he finds even in himself less than he wants, sometimes he grows contemptuous of what he has found. Or else, believing there is nothing more than whatever he has found, he binds himself to it so desperately that he becomes the captive of what he has chosen. Sometimes, too, he simply cannot see what is there because trivial and selfish expectations prohibit entrance to the depths of the self and preclude real experience of the joys of life together. In every case, estrangement from the supremely actual means that the relationship between expectations and actuality has come unglued. Certainly Mauriac is not mistaken in his portrayal of the ways that the human becomes daimonic when we lose perspective upon it and of how strong those daimons are; communities like the family will become structures of destruction if there is no relativizing and qualifying of what we demand from ourselves and others, no recognition that we do not need to pose as gods. Then we are condemned to leave the world of "thou" and dwell on a flat dark plain in the land of "it."

For most of us, though, the passions of Louis and the daimons they sow are beyond imagining; the heroic and the diabolic seem equally and completely distant. There are reasons for this, because our estrangement breeds a new dialectic of its own. What begins as an ecstatic movement beyond the self toward union with some greater power concludes by depriving the self of its own actuality. In other words, the daimons eventually consign us to the hegemony of the everyday world, where we are lived through by others rather than in command of lives of our own, just as Louis' hatred leads him to obsession with every mood and whim of his children, cheated by himself of time and energy ever to be his own man. Then the daimons seem far removed from our situation, but still they are its authors. The artificer of idols discovers that he is not only their servant but that he is also captured by the quiet daimonism of the everyday world. The false ultimates that he has fashioned ineluctably deliver him into its hands: share and share alike. Impotence is the reward that the strength of our passion reaps.

Because the communities and powers that rule our worlds counsel us to define ourselves wholly by our relationships to them, wholly by the roles we play there and the functions we perform, not only do we lose something of ourselves while we inhabit their territory but all of the self seems to disappear as soon as we venture outside. Then we are strangers in a foreign land where no one knows who we are, least of all ourselves. The reason, of course, is that whenever we leave the shelter of our daimons we no longer possess any definition of the self in the name of which to protest against the ways that others define us, and so we are vulnerable to any sort of usage, no matter how random or shallow, and entirely at the mercy of the everyday. The man who builds idols is fated to learn that whenever leisure affords opportunity to leave the precincts of their temples he becomes a protean self, condemned to be as others see him or desire him to be because he has no certainty or real experience of his own identity apart from whatever he has derived from his gods. Wherever the images bought by these relationships are no longer pertinent, there is nothing more substantial to the self than the images it finds reflected in the eyes of others or the sum of whatever it manages to consume. Ironically, indeed, it is the quest of more assured and expansive identity that assaults our own integrity, the appetite for ecstasy that finally dissipates the self in the everyday world, the thirst for an ultimate that produces a protean man, as ephemeral as the momentary desires of those who pass by.

In the realm of the everyday where the other whom I encounter is an "it" and I am an "it" as well, contemporary society takes exquisite vengeance upon all those who experience their identity primarily as consumers, secure in the conviction that the key to happiness lies in what one can chew, swallow, sniff, or drink. But the consumer is himself a commodity in relation to other consumers, dependent on their tastes and on the vicissitudes of fashion. So I will be as you desire me, your wishes will be mine and I promise to be nothing but your wish, and the evidence of how desirable I am will be the agglomeration of commodities for which I have traded the commodity of myself. Protean man, nothing if not "contemporary" and "relevant," finds that there is no sense of the worth of the self or experience of its identity apart from the images of him that others hold. This equation of the self with its appearance is mirrored and confirmed, of course, by our pervasive cosmetic impulse, for the drugstore offers plentiful aids for those who yearn to be born anew, a limitless array of functional equivalents for traditional rites of passage, and more than enough pills that will transform the appearance of reality at the price of no inventiveness or measured scrutiny. In the requiem that concludes *Death of a Salesman,* Charley tells the Loman brothers:

> Nobody dast blame this man. You don't understand: Willy was a salesman. And for a salesman, there is no rock bottom to the life. He don't put a bolt to a nut, he don't tell you the law or give you medicine. He's a man way out there in the blue, riding on a smile and a shoeshine. And when they start not smiling back —that's an earthquake. And then you get yourself a couple of spots on your hat, and you're finished. Nobody dast blame this man. A salesman is got to dream, boy. It comes with the territory.[11]

There was no rock bottom for Willy Loman, nowhere in the self and nowhere in the world, and it is his son whose words provide the best epitaph: "Charley, the man didn't know who he was." Willy Loman had no way of access to himself except in terms of his relationship to the chimerical absolute of "success" or through the images of himself reflected in the eyes of others. When indifference caused their eyes to turn away or when death interrupted the gaze of old associates, by so much was Willy diminished until, when the daimons had finished their work, there was simply nothing at all.

There are two paths that seem to promise release from the

dialectic of estrangement and the recapture of a proper dialectic in our lives and loves. One introduces us to the refuge afforded by the free time that affluence allegedly brings. But free time is an ambiguous affair. It is far less than leisure, which designates an achievement of our own and not simply an accident or something given to us by others. Leisure means that we have managed to put our private stamp upon some hours that belong to no one except ourselves; they are unconventional, in the sense that they have not been shaped by the routines and conventions of the everyday world. Sometimes we employ our leisure to be with others, but this is our free choice; sometimes we prefer to be alone, willing to be with ourselves because we know the difference between solitude and loneliness. There are metaphysical grounds for the bite of loneliness, certainly, because we are made for life together; and yet the pain also suggests that we have lost our appetite for ourselves and mislaid the impulse to map new terrain within the self that there has never been an opportunity to explore. Because leisure tells us that the self is more than its relationships to the communities and powers of the world, its enjoyment suggests that the self has reason to value others as individuals, too, rather than simply to weigh them in terms of their services and roles.

But our everydayness robs us of the appetite to be with ourselves, even if not of selves worth the attempt to be with, and so it clouds our capacity to appreciate the reality of other men. We begin to identify selfhood with externalization and privacy with concealment. Privacy becomes the domain where we do whatever is too eccentric, indolent, or shameful for public display, while the greater the public display, the greater the illusion of selfhood. "They say" triumphs again, and we continue to lose touch with anything distinctively our own. We flee from privacy, then, and spend our free time on shopping for small indulgences and in the continual pursuit of entertainment. The time at our own disposal obdurately remains nothing more than a random agglomeration of hours that we spend for whatever lies within our reach. Our free time is shaped by the context in which we spend the greater part of our lives, and we are returned to the captivity of the everyday by our inability to humanize the resource that originally seemed to offer some promise of release. As a consumer of enjoyment, a person who buys the privilege to be a spectator, man uses his free time merely to confirm the tyrannies, assumptions, and passivity of which he is the victim in his ordinary life. Affluence provides exactly what it promises: just time on our hands, free time, time free and therefore tedious and empty, time that turns upon us and consumes all our time in the struggle to fill it with anything at all.

Free time offers us no reason for hope, then, unless it is converted to more than itself. After all, mobs form because men have time on their hands; the individual emerges from the crowd only if he has leisure. One provides some mild and momentary ecstasy, but the other does nothing to remedy how vulnerable we are, for it is merely an emptiness waiting to be filled by whatever the everyday affords. In the end, our problem is the impoverished imagination that cannot discover how to transform time into leisure. It is impossible if there is no taste for one's own self, for its depths and strangeness and labyrinthine ways, but still the appetite will flicker and wane if it is not provisioned with rich and persuasive images of what it means to be a man. Not all the wishes in the world are powerful enough to alter the human situation. Deprived of imagery that will enable them to recognize and respond to the dimension of depth within themselves, individuals can indulge in endless fantasies about who they really are and what their possibilities might be, and yet refusal to submit to conventional standards and values is an option that remains, quite literally, "unimaginable."

There are many ways we can humanize whatever time we have for ourselves, some of them as arduous and complex as they are important: all our commerce with the arts, the small rituals we devise for the early hours of the morning so that we can pause with ourselves for a bit, times of prayer, moments in the woods when we try to pierce through our own preoccupations and see the real shape of what we confront. At least one strategy, though, is known to every child: I do not simply "fill up" or "spend" my time whenever I begin to play a game or tell myself a story or let imagination bring into sharp relief some detail of my world; time is made different, transformed. Even so, playing is no sufficient remedy for all that ails us, for the everyday realm is not overthrown simply by the creation of a new world at its side, especially when the new reflects the fallenness of the imagination that created it and seems so fragile and temporary beside the solid and inexorable lineaments of the old. What matters is not whether I can export the self to other territory for a while but what I can import to the place where it usually dwells. In other words, our need is not simply for a bit of vacation but for an interpretation of the self as player that can qualify and relativize the understanding of ourselves that we gain from our functions and roles and relationships in the realm of the everyday. But that is more than leisure can provide or justify, for it gains its meaning and savor from its symbiotic relationship to the "serious business" of living.

The other place where a promise of liberation is heard is within a community that claims allegiance to the holy. If leisure will not remedy the gravest consequences of our everydayness, however, it is equally true that the Christian community has its many ambiguities, and these can also inhibit the recovery of health in our faiths, hopes, and loves. The church is part and parcel of the fallen world in which it lives, and the daimons of this greater domain appropriate the imagery of Christian faith in order to maintain their own hegemonies. In other words, the symbols and stories of this tradition are continually expropriated by the voices of family or nation in such a fashion that they now present the self as product instead of project, or the social structure as an absolute rather than a challenge, or the culture as anchored in "the nature of things" instead of a contingent human creation, or the civilization as a fair representation of all the possibilities for ecstasy that the world can offer instead of a finite reality standing beneath the judgment of a God who will someday bring men beyond all the raptures they have experienced hitherto. But the ambiguities of the community are of its own devising, too, and not simply visited upon it by external events. The church is scarcely innocent when it becomes a force for the distortion of the virtues as much as for their encouragement; if we do not trace the whys and ways that it vitiates the realities it claims to nourish, we shall know that much less about the actual range of possibilities at our command.

No account of the idea of virtue will clarify our understanding of ourselves if it ignores the ways that all the elements of selfhood, our instincts and desires, our imagination and reason and emotions, are wounded and disrupted by our fallenness. Nor can exploration of the meaning of the idea ignore the relationship between communal experience and individual identity, as though virtue were something the self could not only achieve for itself but could attain in abstraction from its own particular social history. Obviously enough, the social world plays a decisive role in the process by which the dialectical character of faith, hope, and love is lost, only to be supplanted by a new dialectic that tells of man's estrangement from himself.

It is no less true, of course, that were it not for other selves there would be not even the beginnings of faith, hope, and love. The magnitude of hope depends upon the help of others and on the ways that their imaginations augment our own. The generosity of love depends upon the others who first cherished and affirmed the self despite whatever it said or did. Faith is kindled by the trustworthiness of other people and its maintenance depends upon what others say. So much are we dependent upon others that even our relationship to God depends upon them—and so greatly, too, must they depend upon us. So the riches and dangers of our social experience cannot be satisfactorily weighed in abstraction from the churches that men build, and especially not in abstraction from the particular community that calls itself Christian. At least in the West, it is this tradition that has most loudly and consistently claimed to represent more than social experience and therefore to be capable of offering a promise that social experience itself will never honor, the pledge of release from the daimons of the world and the vise of the everyday. The notion of virtue has a long history of distinctively Christian usage; nothing could be more anomalous than the attempt to speak of it without reference either to what the Christian community is or to what it is intended to be.

5

churches

In the eleventh chapter of Genesis, the origin of the richness and diversity of our languages is described in the story of a tower that men determine to build as high as heaven in order to make a name for themselves. But God confounds their speech in order to affirm his own sovereignty, and so they must cease their building because they no longer understand one another. The name of their tower is Babel. In *The Spire,* William Golding writes of towers that are built not in the land of Shinar but within the household of God. This is the first of three statements about churches that an essay on virtue must not ignore: towers rise on hallowed ground as often as they are built on the plains outside. Jocelin, dean of the cathedral of Our Lady, is possessed, haunted by the image of a frozen rapture, an ecstasy in stone that will rise four hundred feet in the air and crown his church. All his powers are marshaled to fulfill the dream of the spire, for "I have so much will, it puts all other business by."[1] Because the dream is an absolute that fills the horizons and everything in Jocelin is taut as the string of a bow drawn toward its target, the dean has lost all ability to question either his actions or the motives on which he acts, deprived by his own intensity of any perspective and blind to everything except "the dreadful glow of his dedicated will."[2]

"Lost in his private storm,"[3] one day Jocelin cries out to his vision, "I didn't know how much you would cost up there, the four hundred feet of you. I thought you would cost no more than money. But still, cost what you like."[4] The price is everything. The monument to prayer deprives Jocelin himself of the ability to pray. The ambition to add a spire to a cathedral becomes the willingness to trade a cathedral for a spire. Dedication destroys devotion as the candles of the church are extinguished and do not burn again. The spire that begins to soar above the earth robs Jocelin of all human companionship, for "when you build like this, men blunt like a poor chisel or fly off like the head of an axe."[5] Later, much later, he confesses that "If I could go back, I would take God as lying between people and to be found there. But now witchcraft hides Him."[6] The divine as well as the human has withdrawn its presence from a landscape that is all barren except for the daimons that swarm through its streets. What was intended to be a symbol of divine condescension has become nothing more than another expression of the vanity of human aspirations and of their power to devour the self that entertains them.

In the first days of construction, the dean is angered by the filthy songs of the army of his laborers as they track across the nave of the cathedral. But then "other things pushed the contrition out of his head"[7] and soon he is certain that "all small things had been put on one side for him, business, prayer, confession, so that now there was a kind of necessary marriage; Jocelin, and the spire."[8] He becomes one of the laborers himself, fetching and carrying, ignoring all his responsibilities as dean and confessor because of the "overriding necessity that I should abandon everything else to stay with these men."[9] The dream is a *daimon* and, like all of its kind, delivers Jocelin to the servitude of the everyday. The passion for more than the earth condemns him to less, and the grip of the realm of the everyday becomes more and more constricting until the day when the angel-*daimon* in whom he had trusted "put away the two wings from the cloven hoof and struck him from arse to the head with a white-hot flail."[10] But now it is too late, and already there are many others, and not only the dean, for whom "what had once been the whispered expostulations of the spire was now a shouting and screaming with the roar of released Satan as a sort of universal black background."[11] What Jocelin has sown and tended is "a plant with strange flowers and fruit, complex, twining, engulfing, destroying, strangling"[12] the cathedral and its parishioners—Pangall and his wife, Goody, Roger and Rachel Mason, and Jocelin most of all.

The old priest had never admitted even to himself how deep was his passion for Goody Pangall, nor recognized how it found warped expression in the marriage to an impotent custodian of the church that he had arranged for her. He managed to keep her chaste, except where she was kept "down in the vaults, the cellarage of my mind."[13] There is a displacement of the appetite for Goody Pangall involved in the strength of his obsession with his spire, and the two passions that are really a single lust war and merge and then war again with one another.

> "What is it [Jocelin asks an aunt] when one's mind turns to one thing only, and that not the lawful, the ordained thing; but to the unlawful. To brood, and remember half in pleasure, half in a kind of subtle torment—"
> "What thing?"
> "And when they die; for they die, they die; to re-create scenes that never happened to her—"
> "Her?"
> "To see her in every detail outlined against the air of the uncountry—indeed, to be able to see nothing else—to know that this is a logical part of all that went before— . . . It's a kind of haunting. All part of the rest."[14]

Even so, despite the fact that he has been able to glimpse what some of the consequences would be for Goody Pangall and Roger Mason if he refused to halt his construction, it is passion for the spire that triumphs over what it has displaced. Jocelin abandons the girl he once so jealously guarded with the words, "I would protect her if I could—protect all of them. But we are each responsible for our own salvation."[15]

As the hour of death approaches for the dean, he stumbles from his bed to the inn where Roger Mason, with no comfort except alcohol, waits for the spire he has built to collapse and destroy the church beneath it. Jocelin says to him:

> "Once you said I was the devil himself. It isn't true. I'm a fool. Also I think—I'm a building with a vast cellarage where the rats live; and there's some kind of blight on my hands. I injure everyone I touch, particularly those I love. Now I've come in pain and shame, to ask you to forgive me. . . .
> "What's a man's mind, Roger? Is it the whole building, cellarage and all? . . .
> "The trouble is, Roger, that the cellarage knew about him—knew he was impotent, I mean—and arranged the marriage. It was her hair, I think. I used to see it, blowing red about a thin, pale face. . . .

"There ought to be some mode of life where all love is good, where one love can't compete with another but adds to it. What kind of a thing is a man's mind, Roger?"[16]

The tower must fall because there is no human skill that can manage to hold four hundred feet of stone in the air when there are no foundations for it, and when there is no way that they could be driven into the treacherous mud beneath the cathedral. In another sense, of course, the spire has long been fallen, because what foundations it has are driven so deeply into the cellarage of the mind. As the last wave of consciousness gradually begins to ebb, Jocelin "looked up experimentally to see if at this late hour the witchcraft had left him; and there was a tangle of hair, blazing among the stars; and the great club of his spire lifted towards it. That's all, he thought, that's the explanation if I had time."[17] They are there, the spire and the hair, filling the whole range of vision, a hopeless tangle in which neither love for the human nor love for the divine can attain what it seeks; both become daimons born of a single passion that reason could not tame or even chart, "down in the vaults, the cellarage" of the self.

Pangall is murdered, his wife has died in the course of giving birth to a dead child, her lover is cruelly destroyed—so much the spire has cost. For Jocelin himself, a vision has enforced such blindness that he is able to see nothing beyond it except for a girl who has become "a kind of haunting" ever after her death. Within the precincts of the cathedral of Our Lady, its dean has lost the impulse toward companionship without which hope cannot flourish, loved with such strength that passion destroys all vestiges of perspective upon his love, buried himself in his projects until he is robbed of all taste for the actualities of the human, and identified those projects with the will of God until faith can no longer question either the self or its narrow and desperate world. So goes the dialectic of estrangement, except that now it has emerged within the church and not outside: his single commitment betrays Jocelin into the hands of daimons, and the daimons consign him in his new vulnerability to all the coarse and demeaning tyrannies of the everyday. The man who hoped to build a spire that would reach as high as heaven becomes the servant and apprentice of an army of laborers who never raise their eyes from the elements of the earth.

The church is a community of the fallen, always and everywhere a household of Jocelins. It can deafen men to genuine intimations of the holy as well as open their ears, use whatever faith and love men possess for ends unholy and inhuman, subvert everything that first it promised to sustain. In the church we meet ourselves and find little cause for rejoicing at the encounter, because we do not seem much different than we were before. But now we are also the members of another institution, and our situation is all the worse because of that. No institution can heed the Passover injunction, for its drive toward power and prestige is not qualified by other and higher loyalties as it is in the lives of most individuals. Then, too, the church is wedded to a variety of other institutions in many and complex ways; the consequence is that whenever it is not building its own spires it is busy helping to fashion towers that rise toward the sky from other locations within the city of man. So the faith of the individual, unwitting and unwilling though he may be but simply because he is a member of this institution, fattens to include other and more ambiguous versions of faith and love that are condoned and confirmed by alliances that the church has established. In other words, the church is not only a community of fallen individuals but fallen farther because it is an institution, enmeshed in many patterns of institutional interaction. This is the second statement about its nature that must be explored if the actual possibilities that the individual confronts are to be properly assessed.

The Christian tradition, as well as every other church or sect, has always been tempted to identify itself with the holy far more intimately than either appearances or anything else can justify. The more it yields to the temptation, of course, the more justification it finds for the pursuit of still greater authority. At first it seems strange that the world should be so slow to challenge this claim to holiness, but the world is wise because the confusion serves its own instincts for survival even more profoundly than it expresses ecclesiastical presumption. People crave the assurance that the values they serve and the loyalties they pledge are not as ambiguous as the motives that inspire them, or as compromised as the results they manage to achieve, or as evanescent as their own careers. The terrible confusions that lacerate the modern world render even more poignant their thirst for some permanence within the transitory, something inviolable in the midst of an exploitative society, a realm of the sacred beside the profane. It is no small comfort if they can persuade themselves that they are satisfactorily related to the holy simply because they are held within some ecclesiastical embrace.

Churchly claims to sanctity do much more than satisfy the longings of individuals, though. What we call "society" is knitted together by a variety of institutionalized conversations that in greater or lesser measure all reinforce one another, else the fabric of our common life would come unstitched, and together they provide people with a secure and established vision of "reality." But if this "reality" is not to shatter eventually into a million pieces, there will be times when it cannot do without a "sacred canopy" that will render it invulnerable to the acids of doubt or accidents of fortune, secure from disrespect and abusive treatment.[18] In other words, the social order will be victimized by all sorts of contingencies, defenseless against sudden subversion by revolution or slow erosion by skepticism, unless it is widely acknowledged to be founded upon "the way things really are" and befriended by powerful gods.

Churches are important to the reigning powers, then, even more important than their armies, because of the ways that they can enforce patterns of socialization that adjust the individual more satisfactorily within society and assure everyone that the shape of the social world is anchored in "the nature of things" and could not be much different. If men are no longer redeemed from sin and death, at least they are rescued from the fear of anomie. The fortunes of the churches are determined quite simply by the "goodwill" that they generate within the primary institutions of society, and there is nothing upon which this depends, of course, except their social functionality. Not even complete irrelevance will be regarded quite so benevolently as a certain usefulness. What the world requires of its churches is that they should invest the prevailing values and social structures with a timeless and sacred aura. So there is an uncomfortable analogy between the church and the magic mirror that belonged to the wicked stepmother of Snow White; it is the beneficiary of goodwill to the extent that it reflects the image that the culture holds of itself, thereby diminishing the possibility of any serious and critical perspective.

The church is wise and faithful enough to repent of the ways that it is subverted by its own conspiracy with the world. Often it does, protesting that like John the Baptist it is not intended to point toward itself and its alliances but toward another who is still to come. Sometimes there are great discrepancies between its protestations of penitence and its actions, but the common memories that remind it of its birth call the community to recognize once again that it lives only for God and not for the world. So there is a sort of humility about the church even as an institution, and at least intermittently it disavows any authority or power except what is generated by the message it is called to proclaim. Its problem, though, is that a certain humility and disengagement will not bring it back to independence and integrity, much less to influence, in a world shaped by the interaction of institutions. Instead, the church is threatened with greater irrelevance and increased dependence, as well as with the erosion of the resources and authority that it can muster for its struggle on behalf of the wretched of the earth and against the reigning principalities and powers. The limitations that the community imposes upon itself in the name of faith, then, render more difficult the fulfillment of the tasks that faith is called to perform. So the church moves to and fro between greater involvement and greater detachment, between a pursuit of power that separates it from those it is intended to help and a disavowal of power that leaves it helpless against the powers of the everyday.

Christian community has no option except to concern itself with the maintenance of some sort of stable order by the primary institutions of society. If there were no such stability, neither could there be liberty or justice for anyone. Self and social world are mutually dependent; when a person loses that world he has lost himself. No matter what its condition, therefore, the preservation of the social order seems preferable to its dissolution. Despite revolutionary rhetoric, no phoenix rises from the ashes of disorder, and, after all, faith counsels that the holy is the preserver of every world and promises the redemption of them all. Not only is disengagement from the world at odds with faith in God, the church must pursue its own institutionalization if it is to influence the policies and effects of other institutions. Now another dimension of the predicament emerges, however. The church exists to worship the holy and to serve the human in this name, but the world where it dwells is concerned with a different polarity, one that is always important, constantly exigent, even more ancient: cosmos and chaos. There is ineradicable tension between concern to maintain a particular cosmos against the threat of chaos and focus upon the mystery of the holy and the human. Each polarity awards primacy to what is subordinated by the other; each finds its gravest dangers where the other would not search. One cares for the dialectic that faith, hope, and love demand; the other finds its surest support in a subversion of the dialectic that will place the individual wholly at its disposal.

The plight of the church, then, is that it cannot keep faith with the holy if it ignores the problem of cosmos and chaos, but neither can it seem to keep faith if it addresses it. Its relationships with other institutions jeopardize for its members the integrity of faith and hope and love, but it was faith itself that dictated these involvements that compound the fallenness of the community and warp its faith. In other words, the ambiguities of the church are not simply the consequences of its fallenness but also the unavoidable correlates of its proper vocation. It is a mistake, therefore, to believe that whatever ails the church can be remedied by the increase of its faith or the renewal of its love, or even that the grace of God can rescue it from its constant jeopardy. On the contrary, faith is endangered by faith as much as by faithlessness; love is threatened by love and not only by its contraries. This is the third statement about the Christian community that must not be obscured in the discussion of virtue: Fidelity to its own mission is the source of vulnerabilities and problems within the church that render the culture of the virtues more arduous there and their maintenance more difficult. Fallenness is not our only peril. Another chapter will return to this anomaly because, even though there may be no better ground, certainly the church provides very odd soil for those who want to cultivate virtue.

The ancient faiths that appear in some different guise, the new versions of religiosity that populate the earth with still more idols, the various sacralizing tendencies that proliferate in public and private—all testify that in its flight from chaos our society continually lays claim to a holiness that it does not possess and disputes the transcendence of what is genuinely divine. In the eyes of the world, and for very good reason, the worst of sins are "materialism and atheism" because they are the fundamental political deviations, questioning the sacral foundations without which the social order threatens to totter and collapse upon the head of everyone. These are the crimes of which all political opposition is accused, and, of course, from the perspective of the establishment the charge is always valid. Because the church cannot afford indifference toward the business of world maintenance, the focus of its criticism of society changes, too, until it finally manages to convince itself that its principal adversaries also reside in atheism and materialism rather than in the godriddenness that afflicts the world.

So the Christian community becomes one partner in a conspiracy with what it was intended to combat, forsaking the first responsibility laid upon it by the disclosure of the reality that alone is holy, which is the task of exorcizing all the varieties of immanent religiosity that grow so luxuriantly in the soil of our common life. It becomes an important agent for social integration and social control; these are valid and necessary functions, of course, but there remain deep and irremediable tensions between them and some persuasive witness to a power that transcends the world. Most important, this altered focus of Christian criticism has grievous consequences for the progress toward autonomy that the idea of virtue promises. The change deprives the individual of the sort of perspective that is the first requisite if he is to ward off the daimons that haunt the human commonwealth and evade all the forms of cultural piety that hold hidden powers to unman the self. Men look to the wrong quarter, and so they can no longer find their real enemies.

As the church becomes more intimately identified with the institutionalized conversations that sustain the social world, and especially with the most important institutions there, it comes to reflect the social and economic distinctions of its culture—not by its own choice, ordinarily, but simply for the reason of its proximity to some people and its distance from others. The distinctions are reinforced because the investments of the church in the process of world maintenance pay handsome dividends: its members grow more successful in their everyday pursuits or at least more inured to them, because the consequences of participation in the church do not differ much from the results of other forms of socialization. Some parishes serve the rich, others care for the poor, but it is all the same; in one way or another the meaning of Christian community is equated with its instrumental functions for the individual and his society. The manipulative approach to reality that characterizes the secular world is sanctified and encouraged to embrace the holy, too.

One of its expressions is the "politicization" of theology, whether in old Byzantium or by new revolutionaries. Sometimes this is an extension of the concern for world maintenance and sometimes a reaction against it, but in either instance the consequences are equally virulent. The holy is reduced to a patron of the present or future *polis*, poetry is sacrificed for prose, and the richness of the theological vocabulary is bartered for a thin mode of discourse that has only a single dimension. The proper Christian interpretation of the relationship between act and being is simply stood on its head, commitment is wrongly identified with activity in one particular and exclusive context, and faith concerns itself with the human to the exclusion of the divine. Still we talk of the politics of God, though, unaware of the denial of God or of the loss of perspective on politics that our speech involves.

There is a second expression of a manipulative stance toward reality that can also infect the church: The technological achievements of modern culture provide a climate hospitable to magic. Our fascination with power and our illusion that it is an end as well as a means combine with the sense of our own powerlessness, the pervasive suspicion among us now that autonomy and agency have somehow become the characteristics of systems and no longer the attributes of selves. Because a manipulative approach to God seems to find some verification in the results of ecclesiastical processes of socialization, it also seems credible that sacraments and scriptures have a mysterious potency of their own. So possession becomes more important than application, repetition than interpretation, incantation than prayer. No matter whether we submit to the politicization of theology or preside at its declension into magic, the result is the same. We no longer let God be God but place ourselves at the center and him on the periphery, and for that reason our manipulative ventures eventually reduce us to nothing more than instruments in political or religious affairs.

The community that once was described as a pilgrim venture in a foreign land carves out a *polis* for itself and settles down with the native tribes. The individual who first was exalted by his membership in the community is cheated because no longer is he anything more, although a little putative magic offers illusions of relief from the tedium of the everyday. But there is little that the individual can do for himself now, for when a magical or instrumental approach to faith counsels adherence to their "literal" significance, Christian images are divested of their power to provoke men to work for the transformation of the social world. The imagery has simply lost its relevance there and provides no sort of remedy for tribalism. Tribalism does not mean that love is gone, of course, but now love has lost its distinctively Christian character as an act directed toward outsiders and strangers; identity with the tribe dulls the sense of separateness that enables an individual to offer himself in ways that the community does not sanction. Nor does belief in magic signify the disappearance of hope, but hope is no longer directed toward the intrinsic resources of the self and its world or sustained by belief in the agency of the individual; it is entirely dependent now, and so there is nothing it can create. The vocabulary of politics does not involve the rejection of faith, but now faith loses the richness of its interpretive resources and invests itself in idols, binding men to the hegemony of some real or imagined *polis*, stifling their questions about what lies beneath the surfaces of things.

Each distortion confirms and aggravates the next, each tells of the erosion of the dialectical character of a particular virtue. The tribal, the magical, the political—rooted together and entangled with one another, mysteriously growing in soil that was originally tilled in obedience to a commitment at the core of Christian faith, concern for the maintenance and humanization of the social world. Nevertheless, despite all the ways that his relationships to worldly powers and institutions can cripple and demean the individual, and his particular relationship to the church no less than others, it is still impossible to isolate the notion of virtue from the communities without which no faith can endure or hope find satisfaction. There must always be some culture where a certain vision of the world is regarded as indisputable and where provisions exist for the socialization of new generations in accordance with that vision. Our faiths, hopes, and loves are born from and tested in and sustained by social experience; if they are ever to become Christian, this will not occur anywhere except within the church, and nowhere else can their Christian character be maintained.

The fallenness of the church is not an affair that happened once upon a time or once for all, so that there is no longer room within it for whatever is truly human. As Christians understand the matter, the community reflects a mixture of its essential possibilities and of their existential distortion; it is necessary to reckon not only with the frailty and folly of men but also with the power and mercy of God. On the one hand, the church is a community of sinners and a sinful community, and its ambiguities are all the greater because fidelity to its essential vocation leads it into new sorts of jeopardy. On the other, the same presence that launched the church upon its mission comes again to fashion anew its faith, hope, and love until they are directed once more toward the holy and luminous in their witness to the reality and power of God. So the community is called back from the paths marked out by the clamorings of its own ambitions or by the designs of the other institutions on which it depends. The divine renews the human and works within it. The relation between essential and existential is reversed, in the sense that the holy transforms the existential in order to reveal something of its essential and more than human meanings and possibilities. The Bible continually speaks of the condescension of the holy, of the manifold ways in which God identifies himself with and employs fallen human realities so that even in the midst of their fallenness they are enabled to point beyond themselves. The human subversion of the church is subverted in its turn by what God wills the community should be; then new instances of faithlessness demand a judgment and cry out for a redemption that the church can never offer to itself.

This sort of interpretation of the ways of God with man has always lain at the heart of the Christian tradition; whenever it is relegated to the periphery of faith, there is no longer a genuinely theological motive for membership in the church at all. Not only does God insistently search for the outsider, for the enemies and the ungodly, but he uses even their betrayals to implement his own humanizing ends. This, too, is a crucial element in a Christian introduction to the meaning of virtue. In a story by Ernst Wiechert, a widow says to her son, as he is about to set off for the trenches of World War I, "My son, if you bring me honor I shall be proud of you, and if you bring me dishonor I shall always be your mother."[19] So it is that the holy unites itself with a fallen human institution, much as persons identify with one another and yet do no violence to their own integrity.

The holy is more than the human, and it seeks to accomplish renewal and not simply to offer acceptance. Renewal always lies on the far side of judgment, and sometimes judgment is lengthy and painful. But the holy is not less than the human, and so the motive for judgment springs from the depths of its love. The means by which the divine operates are not at all extraordinary. The myths and imagery of the church suddenly display strange new power to capture and ingest the individual, enabling him to act upon loyalties that his own interests would never condone. Or else someone manages to throw off his mood of desperate seriousness about himself and finally escapes the nets of the everyday world because he sees the comic aspects of a universe in which only a single reality is ultimately serious. Or the "theological" virtues are developed within the life of an individual to an extent that curiously surpasses the quality of experience in the church to which he belongs. Or one day the mysterious interiority of others and the unsocialized depths of the self that first kindled faith in the holy are met once more, and we are overwhelmed by the involution of anguish and wonder, sadness and hope, gratitude for gifts received and shame at appointments missed. These things happen because the holy is never content to leave the human alone, or so Christians believe; but much is not visible even to the eyes of faith, and so the knowledge of when and where they will happen, that is a secret.

As a preface to exploration of the dialectic of its mission, one more word must be written about the church. When a person enters the contemporary Christian community, ne identifies himself with a tradition that, at its commencement, was regarded by its adversaries as socially disfunctional in every way. Christians were not persecuted because they added some new ingredient to the Hellenistic stew of pieties; on the contrary, they opposed them all, and most intransigently the ones that contributed most to the maintenance of the body politic. It requires no great sociological perception to recognize that the contemporary church has become one of the most useful institutions in the West, fostering indifference and suspicion toward the outsider or radical, reinforcing distinctions of class and caste, implicated in all sorts of conspiracies to maintain tribalism and the reign of the everyday. There is not much reason for the church to congratulate itself upon its upward mobility.

On the other hand, while the disparity between the social roles of the primitive Christian community and the modern church is a fact that simply cannot be ignored, there is no reason to twist it into a negative judgment upon the tradition, although that is a conclusion all the more tempting because it seems so simple and obvious. Nevertheless, the change does not necessarily mean that the church has lost touch with its origins and true vocation—except, of course, to the extent that it burdens faith in God with a weird and weighty freight of cult loves and culture loyalties. Because the mission of the church is a genuinely dialectical affair, reaching in different directions that initially seem incompatible, it can be pursued no matter where the church stands.[20] Especially in a time of social change without parallel, the tradition stands to betray itself by any unambiguous commitment to either conservation or revolution, either legacies of the past or promises of the future.

Whenever the dialectic is maintained, the community can conserve its heritage and defend itself against the dangers of the new alliances and entanglements in which the church has become involved. If it is lost, however, Christian faith is defenseless against its own exclusiveness and tribalism, and its new situation becomes a betrayal of all the twisted and wretched and hopeless inhabitants of the earth. Where the inner dialectic of its vocation is understood and obeyed, the church affords a context where faith, hope, and love can express their own dialectical character. They find new amplitude and strength because their situation is hospitable to the culture of the "classical" virtues of temperance and justice, prudence and courage—the resources without which men are relegated to immaturity and wrong sorts of dependence, no matter how strong their faith, sacrificial their love, or bright their hope. Without these, there can finally be no virtuous or Christian life worth the name. One of the lessons that the church is intended to teach is that Jew and Greek are not meant to live apart from one another. One side of the Mediterranean will not survive without the other—and there is a dialectic in this, too, at least when it touches moral life. If they meet, however, they will be introduced by someone who is a stranger to them both. Quite literally, the stranger provides the indispensable clue if we are ever to recognize that someone else is real.

6

strangers

The account of judgment at Babel is a prelude to the disclosure of the mercy of the holy at Pentecost, when the words of a hundred different languages are marshaled in common service of the Word of God. "Devout men from every nation under heaven," we are told, were amazed because each heard the disciples "telling in our own tongues the mighty works of God." Peter raises his voice and begins, "Men of Israel, hear these words," and when his narrative of the Christ is done, "they were cut to the heart, and said to Peter and the rest of the apostles, 'Brethren, what shall we do?'" (See Acts 2:5, 11, 22, 37.) The import of the story is that the characteristic mode of divine activity involves the use of what is fallen, so that even in the midst of its existential distortion some of its essential possibilities to be transparent to its source are achieved. The tribalism of language that reflects both human pride and divine recompense is overcome so that words can again express the universal relevance of the Word of God.

Christian faith is born of listening; it is a response to the speech of other people who talk with us about God. Listening provides us with our first and final intimation of transcendence, for the experience of the speech of someone else acquaints us with a reality that is hidden behind and beneath the words. There is a strangeness, an enigma, something unfathomable at the source of the most familiar and banal language, and words give us no full access to whatever dwells there. This transcendence is an ambiguous phenomenon, of course; often we become aware of it in a moment when we recognize that another person is lying to us, and so it generates distrust and suspicion. Still, it provides a reason to try to listen to persons and not simply to their speech, and sometimes the presence of this self that is never fully present in its words offers a scrap of verification of the Christian message about a holy reality that transcends the human condition. *The church, then, is first of all an instance of speaking,* one example among many of the most common human act, an event that is sometimes peremptory or slovenly or abusive, sometimes deeply revelatory, but which is the beginning of everything else. The church understands itself as able to speak, though, only because it is a faithful hearer; when it no longer listens to its author it deprives itself of anything to say. Speaking and listening are bound inseparably to one another, at least in the life of this particular community. They are bound inseparably in another way, too, and this is the source of the jeopardy in which the church is placed by its vocation; not only must it listen faithfully if it is to proclaim the Word of God, it is constrained also to listen to those to whom it speaks.

Words serve us in many ways; their primordial function, however, is not to communicate meanings to someone else but to enable persons to grasp and shape the texture and meanings of their own lives. Language is the instrument by which we organize the continuum of our experience, investing it with a certain permanence, sifting it to discover patterns in much that first seemed random, summoning one or another sort of world from chaos. We are aware of much that we have no words to describe, of course, but we come to know only what we can name; language places experience at the disposal of the intellect. It brings us to ourselves and then confronts us with the mystery of the ways that we transcend ourselves. But words are also used to communicate with others, and so they lead us into a public world of shared memories and anticipations where our own interpretations of experience are sometimes corrected, sometimes amplified and confirmed, sometimes falsified and trivialized. The linguistic coinage we inherit is vast, and vast are its possibilities for either more discriminating commerce with reality or the atrophy of intelligence and imagination. Words can be used in many ways and for many ends. For better as well as for worse, what one says and how it is said are shaped by the conventions and expectations of the public worlds where we come to dwell and from which we garner a certain identity as members of this age, this group, this culture.

The people who become "significant others" in our lives are

the ones who finally determine which of these possible worlds we shall inhabit, what our vocabulary and store of images and patterns of linguistic usage will be, and therefore how we shall come to terms with reality. Speech provides the possibility, even if not the certainty, of movement from the realm of "it" into a new world where the self is expanded and enriched because someone else addresses it as "thou." When this occurs, the self finds its identity as an individual and not simply as a member of a group. Those with whom we sometimes manage a relationship of I and thou are, of course, the most important among our significant others, but there are still more of them who never participate in this sort of intimate relationship. Teachers and statesmen, television personalities and employers, the long dead and the not yet born—with these and many others the self can have frequent and influential conversations, or else their standards and expectations are so fully appropriated that they are represented in the internal dialogues of the self with itself. Sometimes we draw more of them from fiction than from life; even so, on these conversations depend the existence and endurance of the particular worlds in which we live. If the dialogues are interrupted, the landscape turns forbidding and strange. So the death of a loved one quite literally shakes the world, and sometimes it is not senility but wisdom that counsels the aged to talk to themselves. Even a journey away from home can breed a sort of metaphysical terror, suggesting that reality is inhospitable now and evermore. When a man must live in a strange land, there are few occasions for such rejoicing as a chance to hear his own language spoken again, for the presence of the speaker indicates that the world does not have a new face and that old assumptions and anticipations are valid still.

No version of faith or vision of man and his world will survive if it is not shared by others—not by all others, of course, but by a number of significant others who constitute a plausibility structure within which men confirm the beliefs of their neighbors. To repeat again what must be a consistent refrain, the faith of the individual is never an individual affair, for all its nourishment comes from sharing and being shared. In this sense, at least, the Lutheran doctrine of the priesthood of all believers is entirely true. In our time, men seem to live in various plausibility structures, and there are often conflicts among them, too, even though few pretend to offer architectonic visions of the earth. More often than not, their confirmation of "the nature of things" is partial, temporary, and never secure from challenge. Some of these communities are entered simply because people are thrown there by accidents of birth or education, class or caste; there are others, though, and churches are among them, in which an individual cannot long remain without some decision of his own. Obviously, plausibility structures tend to exact affirmative decisions. The vocabulary and images of the Christian community, for example, are intended to interpret experience in a fashion that points faithfully toward the disclosure of the holy in Jesus Christ. When men understand and rely upon this tradition for the interpretation of their lives, experience will afford some modest verification of the imagery, never verification beyond dispute but still enough to reinforce the power of the plausibility structure to confirm its own validity.

The function of the church is best described in terms of a priesthood charged with the task of mediation between God and man. Mediation does not mean that the church stands between them, however, as though it were a third party; as ancient theologians said, the world is capable of bearing the hand of the Father. Christian community does not exist in order to afford the world a means of access to God, but to point toward and interpret the ways that God finds his own access to it in his sovereign freedom and mercy. Its vocation is not to give something to others as much as it is to nurture what has already been given to them by powers greater than its own. The church is simply the part of the world that is provisioned to interpret the deepest dimensions of experience that everyone shares. The greatest gift that it offers is the gift of sight, and this more expansive vision provides the self with a new and larger world within which it is free to choose and act in ways that were impossible when it inhabited more confined and confining space.

In other words, the church is a mediator primarily in the sense that it is the guardian of a tradition of stories, myths, and images that serve to weave the cloth of common life in such a fashion that we can recognize intimations of God and learn to worship and serve him. Divine activity does not advertise itself as such. Nor will it often be recognized for what it is by someone unprepared for the encounter, partly because our store of imagery is too impoverished and banal, partly because of our fascination with daimons and idols, partly because our ineradicable selfishness blocks sight of what can be seen only by unselfed regard. Only if we begin with God will we end with him. He is eternally the father of the Christ, however, and therefore his contemporary work displays the same Christic shape that marked his activity with earlier generations. So the common memories on which the church is founded provide keys that are indispensable if men are to grasp the mystery of the presence and activity of God in their histories today.

Scriptures, liturgies, and sacraments, then, provide people with the concrete acquaintance with the way of the Christ that enables them to recognize him as he comes and comes again to the world that he has claimed for himself. They function in much the same way as frequent visits to the home of a friend; familiarity adds to our store of knowledge and power of appreciation, initiating us to the endless complexity of the reality we confront. These sacraments and liturgies also call us to reflect upon the great moments of living and dying, when depths appear beneath the surfaces of things and the clamor of the world recedes until sometimes a small voice is audible again and the urgency of repentance floods the mind. So they perform two services, pointing us toward where we are most gravely questioned and affording us a way to recognize whether we have an appointment there with what is more than human. This imagery is also imbedded in our art and literature and civil religion, of course, but books and paintings require no decisions because people are simply grasped by new worlds. Wherever the Christian message is heard, however, it creates a *krisis* for the social world in which the individual lives and he is forced to decide whether he will continue to understand himself in its terms or in the new ones that are offered to him now.

What threatens the Christian community most grievously is that its proper vocation and not only its fallenness causes it to admit those old worlds to its own universe once again. If the significant others with whom we converse could all be chosen from within the church, then the life of faith would be very smooth, indeed. But the language of the Bible leaves no shadow of a doubt that the mission of the church is to venture continually into terra incognita, to leave home, to seek out the stranger and speak with him. The church is not only an instance of speaking, therefore; unlike all other communities, *it is intended to be essentially an instance of speaking with strangers.* This is the second element in the dialectic of its vocation. No one can escape the necessity to speak with strangers; all of us do it many times in the course of an ordinary week. But for the church, the speaking as well as the listening that it involves is not intended to advance the interests of the community but those of the stranger himself; it is meant to achieve his liberation, his health, the expansion of his possibilities. The church is a mission, then, not in the sense that it is steadfastly intent upon the number of conversions it can score but for the more important reason that it can never escape from the imperative to speak with strangers, except at the price of a denial of its own nature.

There are many tensions between the exigencies of this vocation and the task of mediation, but there is also a profound and dialectical relationship. The obligation to speak with strangers is not a demand laid upon the community from outside, externally. Instead, it is the only way in which the community can disclose its own real nature and affirm what it essentially is. The church is a people that was no people, strangers in a strange land, still walking in the wilderness where it spent its first forty years; in the letter to the Romans, Paul characterizes his brothers as those who were befriended while they were yet strangers, enemies, helpless, ungodly. In the act of speaking with strangers, the church advertises whence it came, what it is, what the intentions of God are toward all men. In other words, the church meets itself, what once it was and what it still remains. It meets itself as the outsider and the twisted and the vicious, as the oppressed and desperate and dissident.

The rewards of these meetings are various and rich, at least from the perspective of faith itself, and in them the church finds opportunities to transcend the limitations that it has imposed upon itself because of its alliances with the powers and principalities that seem to rule the earth. Its heritage constrains it to search for the stranger, and in the encounter the community can learn again the meaning of its heritage. The stranger meets us in many guises, of course, but from each of them faith can draw forth some lesson, if only a deeper sense of the strangeness that lies within ourselves, counseling that we can be more than we are and are more than the ways that the world defines us. It is the presence of the alien, not the familiar faces of family or friends, that provokes the most creative and therapeutic of our encounters with ourselves, because in him I meet someone who is not simply an extension of my own reality. Just for that reason, no impulse is more deeply written into the dynamics of human community than our xenophobia, our pervasive animosity toward strangers. Certainly the church is not immune to it; too often we label the unfamiliar as deviant and evade the lessons it can teach, accomplishing nothing by our labels except the expression of how we will to perceive ourselves and how we refuse to see ourselves at all.

One way that the stranger comes to us is in the form of the retarded child, a little boy who is utterly and irremediably useless, and whose presence means scandal and torment for a utilitarian and manipulative world. Perhaps we have heard that we are valued in ways that are not dependent upon human strengths and purposes, but now the lesson is made flesh and guttural sounds that first seem to express nothing but sweat and pain finally communicate with great clarity

> that all men have significance beyond what they can be for us—our friend, our playmate, our brother; each of us is precious and significant because his being is grounded in God's care. . . . Thus to see the retarded honestly is to remind ourselves that we cannot earn significance for our lives; it is a gift of God. . . . The more that Christians consider the fundamental issues raised by the care of the retarded, the stranger they will feel as they go about amid the glories and ruins of their own building. As we live with such strangeness, perhaps we will be better able to comprehend and love those who exist as strangers among us; they cannot understand as we understand, but these retarded brothers are no less members of God's kingdom.[1]

Useless he is, and weak because whatever power he has is not at his own disposal; but there is something in this frailty that is analogous to the weakness of a God whose only son dies on a cross. Our fascination with power is reflected even in our disavowal of power, for the disavowal itself becomes a new strategy for the control of other people, sometimes more destructive than force because "it has the form of a renunciation of power that controls completely since it does not appear to control at all."[2] But in this boy who must struggle to speak even his own name, and in God, there is a weakness that "lures us from our pretentious attempt to make our lives meaningful through power and violence," or through their renunciation, and calls us to yield ourselves and our world into greater hands.[3] The weakness tells, too, that the God of the biblical tradition is no more the God of our order than of our disorder. He is beyond the distinction, a stillness and a whirlwind that are dangerous partners in our ventures at world maintenance and the ruination of all our theodicies.

The retarded child is a judgment on our loves, on the selfishness of creatures whose loves are motivated by their own needs and whose deepest need is the need to be loved. This boy who will never understand the occasion he presents for loving can scarcely satisfy the possessiveness of our passion, for his incomprehension baffles our dependence on the recognition by others that they are in need of ourselves. He can be affirmed only by a love that does not seek to possess because it knows the utter hopelessness of the desire, and therefore the child begins to command from us a nonpossessive regard. There is nothing that he can do for me, no real ways in which he can respond to me; he must remain obdurately other than I am, a strangeness in our midst. This one can accomplish nothing, except that in his uselessness he can do so much, judging and reforming the selfishness of our love and vision, teaching something of the ways of God with man, reminding us of the remarkable strangeness in everyone and how it eludes measurement by the canons of a fallen world, bringing us by the coarse rope of his strangeness back to new meetings with ourselves. In some ways most important of all for moral reflection, by his incomprehension and inability to live as others do, the boy can finally force us to admit, despite ourselves, that someone else is real. Unteachable himself, he teaches the church.

There are other sorts of strangers who are quick to speak, of course, and often their complaining or argumentative voices assault the self until it is deafened to everything else. Their words sometimes communicate much less than the thickened tongues of the retarded, but always the church must reckon seriously with their views. People are not really loved if their allegiances are too quickly dismissed; the dismissal indicates the absence of humility in one's own relationship to the truth, and where love is not married to humility it is less than love. Even in the instance of a parent confronting a nasty child, there is reason for humility before the odd and simple *being* of someone else. The Christian community is called not merely to speak *to* strangers but to speak *with* them, and if their own understanding of their situation is slighted, no matter how simplistic or freighted with illusion it may be, the church has not grasped who they actually are, for their understanding is not an adjunct to their reality but the power that makes them whatever they are. So nothing is more important than the way that Christian speaking consistently displays a willingness to listen. The readiness to listen, however, endangers the plausibility structure on which faith depends, not only because of the intrusion of alien perspectives but even more because significant others suddenly appear outside the camp and are no longer recruited from within the community. Then foreign doubts are sown alongside native breeds of faith and nourished by the continuation of these new conversations, and therefore the whole of reality threatens to come unstitched.

The exigencies of its mission shape and threaten every aspect of the life of the church. If the stranger is to confront the Christian message, it must be presented in some fashion that is intelligible to him in the midst of his strangeness. But the continual reinterpretation that this involves can never be accomplished without some polarization of the community. Those who are comfortable with an earlier version of faith will find in reinterpretation a threat to their identity as well as a betrayal of the original message. Sometimes, too, the situation may require some quite new form of statement that can serve the strangers as a functional equivalent for the traditional affirmations. This sort of strategy emphasizes the original value of the message as a conveyer of meaning, but it certainly diminishes confidence in its contemporary importance as a conveyer of truth. More important still, if the situation of the stranger within "a rational and functional universe" is to be actually addressed, if the church is to speak concretely to the problems of the desperate and vicious, it seems that mythic language must be supplanted by prose. After all, problems need rational analysis and prescription. It is necessary to clarify what the implicates of traditional symbols and stories really are, what inferences can legitimately be drawn from them, what resources they offer for proximate solutions to contemporary crises.

But this movement from one mode of discourse to a different one always holds the danger that the two will simply fall out of significant relationship. Then, too, it leads us away from the only resource that we have for the discovery of what God is doing, because we now grow unfamiliar with the images that identify who we are, justify the depth of our social concern, and enable us to decipher traces of the divine. So the grip of the everyday is scarcely loosened but may, indeed, merely be reinforced by vague religious imperatives. If some of the meanings of justice can be conceptualized, the works of love can be captured only by poetry, for love is always an imaginative act. If prose will serve for predictions of the future, only imagination can use the future as a power for the transformation of the present. The road that begins with moral imperatives and ends at the entrance to a new world is long and arduous, and without poetry it simply cannot be traversed at all. Injunctions must be captured in images that grasp the attention of the individual and arrest the flux of his experience, so that he can visualize himself as an agent acting in behalf of these particular ends. His deeds will not transcend the constraints of his situation unless they are prompted by images of the self that are more liberated and expansive than the situation itself would admit. The greatest trouble with the church is neither that its members lack goodwill nor that they are bereft of any notions of what ought to be done. Instead, they suffer from the often fatal disease of bleached imagination, and the illness is integrally bound up with the ways that the community is faithful to what its mission toward the stranger demands.

When the church is approached from the perspective of its dialectical vocation, it is possible to offer some answers to at least two perennial questions. First, if Christian community is a principal instance of the grace of God in our world, how can there be so much that is graceless about it? Second, how is it possible to account for such gracelessness except in terms of the absence of faith? Speaking with strangers is a vocation that is never free from anguish. It precipitates a crisis for the church as culture, because there is antagonism no less than a dialectical relationship between the role of plausibility structure, or the task of mediation, and the imperative to speak with those outside the camp. Because Christian systems of symbols direct attention toward the fulfillment of the outsider rather than to the designs of the community, because significant others therefore become the ones who stand outside the sanctuary, because speech is Christian only when it also listens or else we lose touch with the reality of those with whom we converse, a curious anomaly appears in the life of the church: the reason for its existence jeopardizes its existence. The more faithful it is, the more faithless it seems destined to become, because it undermines its own power as plausibility structure. On the other hand, the betrayal of its mission to strangers would deprive the church of contact with its own essential nature and origins.

Its vocation also precipitates a crisis for the church as institution, because there is conflict as much as complementarity between the responsibility in the process of world maintenance which it originally assumes for the sake of the wretched of the earth and its ability to sustain that commitment to the loner and the rebel despite its institutional entanglements. The crises are all the greater because of the reticence that listening involves and the humility that is required by its witness to what lies beyond itself, for humility as well as ambition can deliver it into captivity to the institutions that govern the fallen world. Little that is of real moral or theological interest can be understood about the Christian community if it is forgotten that the church is both enemy and servant of the holy, enemy because it is a community of sinners and a sinful institution, but enemy first of all precisely because it is faithful as a servant, reticent and humble, forgetful of self and committed to the will of its lord. It is betrayed by its own hands because in greater or lesser measure it has kept faith with its essential vocation and has not abandoned it in the search for some easier way. Fidelity always raises new and more subtle possibilities for faithlessness. At least as it understands its own situation, however, the church is not left alone in its attempts to keep faith, for God comes to use its disarray and defenselessness as new occasions to heal blind eyes and open the ears of the deaf—and the roles that the stranger plays in this drama are crucial.

Speaking with strangers does not mean that the community must surrender the task of mediation and become a society of free thinkers, characterized by the false egalitarianism that is vulnerable to any bit of nonsense heard through an open window. On the other hand, its debate with the stranger does not concern what he sees but why he sees the way he does. The church does not first of all contest what he believes but rather the seriousness with which he regards the self that believes. The issue is not so much belief but perspective, not one perspective or another but the need for a perspective that is *unselfed*. The first task of the community, therefore, is to lift from strangers their desperate burden of seriousness about themselves, for this is the root of selfishness and it conflicts irremediably with faith that one reality alone is ultimately serious and that everything else is unserious and often comic in comparison with its source.

This sort of seriousness is bred when men must live outside a realm of basic trust, or when their fundamental trusts are shattered by some event that suddenly invests familiar places with a strange and frightening shape, so that now the lonely self is vulnerable to all sorts of accidents and contingencies and must walk constantly armed. The function of the church is to provide a realm of basic trust where men are liberated from some of their concern for themselves. No longer need they fear to be vulnerable, for they know themselves to be protected and cherished by more than human power; so they can offer themselves to others instead of merely offering their conventional images of themselves, throw away badges of status and come out from behind their mechanisms of defense. Where there is the basic trust that qualifies our seriousness and selfishness, the church can become a genuine *forum*, a place of stillness and silence where persons can listen to the voices within themselves as well as to the words of others and of God.

One of the most noxious forms of pollution in the modern world is noise, above which the individual can often neither make himself heard nor hear himself as he is continually assaulted by music in stores, horns on the highway, crowds and planes and the drone of technology. As all sorts of new versions of religiosity take root in the human commonwealth, the Christian community is intended to be one place where men are set free from the ideological baggage and shibboleths that haunt them, and from either secular or sacrosanct politicizations of theology, so that they can speak and be heard as individual men. The development of institutional autonomy within the social world, the manipulative nature of the mass media, the unprecedented rapidity of generational change, the lies of which our government never wearies, and the hegemony of crowd culture—all testify that the maintenance of a real forum is as crucial a service as it is subversive of the institution that supports it. The forum threatens to mire the church in everydayness and blur the distinctiveness of its message; and yet, precisely because of the ways that it contributes to the task of mediation with which the community is charged, it can finally provide some verification of the promise that "he who loses his life for my sake will find it (Matt. 10:39)."

All sustained dialogue creates and depends upon a conviction of basic trust, but what the church offers differs in important ways from what the family or groups of peers can provide. There is always need for vigilance, of course, for it is so easy to betray what mutuality demands, and more often by thoughtlessness than design. Even so, the basic trust that the community claims to nurture cannot be dissolved by the folly or betrayals of those who are partners there, for it is founded on the Christian assumption that it will be sustained by powers other than its own. For those who are socialized to believe in a power beyond themselves, therefore, betrayal need not be understood as a foreclosure of possibilities; instead, it can furnish an occasion for repentance and forgiveness in which loss is transmuted into gain. The gesture of reconciliation does more than mend what has been torn; in the mending new possibilities emerge, and the old relationship gains a dimension that it did not possess before. So there are even greater opportunities for candor, for the surrender of defenses and acceptance of vulnerability, than the ones that occur within the family or among peers where the welfare of others depends so much upon the integrity of the self. There is escape from the exclusiveness of those communities, too, for in the encounter with strangers the self finds itself challenged and judged in ways that are not common in more familiar preserves. The assumptions and perspectives of others who are alien to us can call forth repentance for our own frequent and despairing dogmatism, and their presence can unself our regard if it calls to a penitent mind the magnitude and meaning of our indifference to strangers in the past.

In these meetings, people are afforded opportunities to encounter depths in other selves that kindle a responsive chord in hitherto unknown or else forgotten depths of their own selves, luring them beyond familiar roles and images of what the self is, redeeming them from the alienation that society enforces. All the vitality of faith hangs upon the frequency of these meetings and the attentiveness of the self to them. What is necessary, of course, is not that others offer verbal confirmation of our faith but rather that in our transactions together they furnish us with the varieties of experience that can illuminate and support the imagery on which faith depends. Either the images will atrophy in their dislocation from experience or else they will grow warped apart from some forum where diverse perspectives combat the tribalism and everydayness that infect every establishment and culture. This is what a plausibility structure really describes when it is concerned not only with a world view but with what undergirds every world view, with a commitment informed by passion and loyalty and trust—not simply a realm of common discourse but a community of shared experience. So the forum that initially threatens to subvert the church eventually proves its best foundation, except for the power of God: the presence of strangers initiates us in new ways to the depths of the humanness we share with them, and tarnished images shine.

It is most often within the context of personal relationships that the self encounters the power that can grasp and shake its foundations in mingled judgment and renewal. It is especially within some realm of basic trust, secured from dissolution despite all the ways in which men wound and torment each other, that personal relationships deepen and expand until they can sometimes testify to the reality of God. Men will find neither time nor inclination to cultivate temperance or justice or courage apart from fields preserved by assumptions of basic trust, but the assumptions cannot be long maintained if temperance and justice and courage are not encountered in our transactions with other selves. In the church, however, where trust is justified by belief in what is greater than man, shared memories of the origin of the tradition furnish images that enable the self to discover analogies and confirmations of divine activity in its experiences of power that can bring forth good from evil, unite the separated, return loyalty for betrayal.

If the first intimation of the holy occurs in the common experience of transcendence involved in listening to another who addresses the self as "thou," perhaps not frequently but so memorably that it leaves an afterglow to color our future commerce with other selves, this is not our only intimation. There is another, at least for the eyes of faith, when we are confronted by the stranger, someone whose presence lends weight to words that tell us there is truth our eyes cannot see, good that evades our partial perspectives, and something stubbornly and finely human that eludes our techniques of manipulation. His presence can call to mind the alien who dwells within ourselves, transcending our understanding and resisting domestication and challenging us to move away from our routinized and comfortable ways in search of the splendid far territory from which we have become emigrants and exiles. If we grant fair play to the stranger, if we can manage to give him a fair hearing, it may happen that we will be called beyond him in obedience to another voice. But there will be no other voice if we offer him less, nothing but the clamor of the daimons again.

What temperance and justice and courage join together to counsel is, we have said, fair play, fairness toward all the possibilities that lie within us and all the actualities that reside in the world. These virtues depend upon more than themselves, however, for they do not know how to begin until the self slowly learns to see what there is that cries out for justice, or is blighted by intemperance, or cannot be met without courage. It is the stranger, not the familiar people whose vision has dictated our own as much as we have molded theirs, who can sometimes force us to confront the formidable but fascinating truth that something or someone else is real, standing against us and resisting us and, as in the instance of the retarded child, commanding an unselfed regard. The gift the stranger brings to the self is the knowledge that the world is not my own creation, that others are as real as am I, and that they are as different from me as my own strangeness is from my ordinary and routinized ways.

Speaking with strangers will always endanger the community, but the church can never do less and still remain a church. Its fidelity jeopardizes itself and invites faithlessness, and so the Christian community seems a very odd place to choose, a particularly unsafe location, for the culture of virtue. But the source of all virtue is an unselfed regard, a reformation of perspective, and for this we must depend upon the strangers whom our xenophobia refuses to admit to the communities and institutions that shape our social world. The alien is not merely an embarrassment or exotic presence imported to amuse us; he can also be the occasion for a new encounter of the self with itself that will heal some of the illnesses that afflict our sight. But we must take him to ourselves and affirm him in his strangeness, for he does not divulge his lessons before the casual glance of those who pass by, and our xenophobia offers no place for these meetings unless there is room for them in the church.

Christian community cannot abandon its task of mediation

when it turns to the stranger, of course, for then it will no longer recognize his importance and have no reason to approach him at all; nor will it have anything of importance to offer to him. It will have forsaken the images that are crucial for the illumination of the ways that his experience with us and ours with him supports and confirms the heritage that the images express. If we turn away from him, though, the images all go sour and we lose touch with the essential nature of our own community, with the mystery of the ways of God, and with the strangeness in ourselves that renders the pursuit of virtue important and the defense of the self against definition in terms of the world a cause too precious to betray. If the dialectic is sustained in our faith and hope and love, as well as in our vocation, the source of its health we shall believe to lie beyond ourselves, and as the images of faith grow more luminous and the presence of the stranger initiates us more fully to the meaning of unselfed vision, perhaps we shall see new traces of the reality in which we believe.

PART THREE

7

temperance, justice, and courage

Along with faith, hope, and love, accounts of Christian moral life have included four other virtues that were regarded by some traditions within classical culture as the ingredients of human fineness.[1] It is important to be able to argue that there is nothing arbitrary about the inclusion of these "cardinal" virtues or about the reluctance to award equal significance to some other possibilities. Temperance, justice, courage, and prudence are the principal elements that are involved whenever man becomes his own master, and the attainment of each ushers the self into a new and crucial sort of freedom. Faith, hope, and love speak of the *gifts* that the self receives from others and of the *dependence* that life involves; the others tell partly of the *achievements* that man must realize by himself and of the *mastery* that life demands. But if the two constellations of virtue can be distinguished from one another, it is nonetheless an error to separate them. Their mutual dependence testifies, as Josef Pieper notes, that "in the Christian era there is no such thing as 'purely natural' virtue without actual reference to the order of grace."[2] When man is not his own master, it is all the more difficult for him to acknowledge in faith and love the sovereignty of God. When divine sovereignty does not enable man to become his own master in some new sense, the holy is the enemy instead of the sustainer of the human. Each of the "cardinal" virtues offers its own witness that he who loves his life will lose it, therefore posing a question that is ultimately theological, and everyone who acts consistently in accordance with justice and courage and temperance finds new reason to acknowledge that he is much indebted to powers beyond his own.

Temperance has traditionally been considered last among the virtues, because it is directly concerned with the self alone while all the others look beyond the individual. But there are several ways in which the distinction is misleading. First, intemperance is a selfish obsession with one's own desires that eventually populates the world with daimons whose grip is no less formidable because the chains have been forged by the prisoner himself. Temperance brings liberation from these phantoms and illusions of the night. Its meaning is *mastery of the self*. It describes the discipline without which the self is not at its own disposal but is, instead, thrust first one way and then another by the various and conflicting fears and desires that lie within ourselves. In other words, it means that now the whole is in command of the parts, no longer subject to the tyranny of what is only a single aspect of the self or else to a succession of different captivities. It enables the self to be alone, alone at last, and with itself whole. Second, temperance is essentially a form of justice, as Plato recognized. Even though it is directed toward the self, it tutors the individual in what justice toward others involves, so that justice will not be confused with indulgence and thoughtless gratification. It supports courage, too, because it provides the reasons for our resistance of others when their demands are intemperate in ways that preclude real justice for them or for ourselves. The "cardinal" virtues are at least as closely bound up with one another as are our faiths, hopes, and loves.

There is nothing puritanical about temperance; it is never guilty of the tedious admonition that everything, perhaps even loving God, ought to be done in moderation. In fact, moderation is nothing but a bourgeois surrogate for the classical notion of temperance, and a particularly vicious substitution because it offers a quantified answer to a fundamental question about the quality of life. Temperance cares only for the quality of experience, though, for the presence in it of a richness and a resonance that reflect the wholeness of a person all of whose powers find their integrated expression. So it never counsels the self to retreat from the riches of the world lest they prove too seductive; its business is to order what lies within the self so that the world can be most deeply and expansively enjoyed. It never says that a man should accept less than his nature craves; instead, it is meant to prepare him so that he can savor many different things and never want less than all he is potentially able to desire. Unconcerned with what is moderate or immoderate, uncaring about the mere intensity or duration of experience, temperance aims at an amplitude in our existence that will mirror and engage the entirety of the self.

The problem of temperance is that nature is disordered and the phantasmagoria of our desiring eludes the nets of the mind. We are uncertain of what it is that we really want, unsure that there are any continuities in the incessant clamor of our desiring, disbelieving that a prize with the taste of ashes could have seemed to promise such rapture when it was pursued a year ago. So temperance cannot stand alone; like love, it needs a wisdom that it cannot offer to itself. We do not know what we describe when we speak of the command of the whole over the parts; we have lost touch with the meaning of wholeness because we can no longer harmonize the dictates of the impulses toward self-affirmation and self-transcendence that shape the dynamics of our lives. Although the relationship of the human to the holy has been ruptured and man has no power to heal it, still the self is endowed with a nature that can find fulfillment only through love for its source. So there is no way that man can kill the appetite for union with what is greater than the self, with what can bring the self to greatness. Temperance must reckon with the existential separation and conflict between two different impulses that have lost their essential unity, as well as with the distorted ways in which each is now exercised.

Because the holy continues to call man beyond himself in penitent rapture, social experience can do much less to vitiate the yearning for self-transcendence than it can to gut the drive toward self-affirmation. If the first desire is not satisfied in one way it will express itself in another—if not in the holy, then in the human; if not in the family, then with peers, corporation, or state; if not through encounters with others, then in the everyday "sharing" of situations where windowless monads are collectively deafened by music or stunned by television; if not in the realm of the actual, then by entrance to the world of fantasy that drugs can manipulate. Each adventure provides its oblique and clouded witness that the creature is endowed with a nature that must love God more than itself and that men will succumb to divinities of their own devising if there is no authentic revelation. Every unqualified identification of the self with something beyond itself is intemperate, of course, but these will occur inevitably apart from a greater faith than the powers of the world can provide, because without a greater faith there will be no images of man on which to build a protest against total commitments.

Sometimes our strategies for self-transcendence are selfish; sometimes they are not. Even when the individual wants nothing except the opportunity to serve a cause greater than himself, however, it is still true that in the search to find his life he has lost something precious in it. The self is buried in a world where its own deepest impulses are unfulfilled, and yet it is an accomplice in its own burial, betrayed by its essential nature to hunt for ultimate fulfillment and betrayed by its existential plight to see nowhere it can find what it desires except within the social world. No longer is the self its own master, then, not because it yields to what is greater than itself but because there is nothing in the world so great that it can respect all the impulses and actualize all the possibilities of a creature who is made in the image of God. Contemporary social experience compounds the danger of the loss of the self through our adventures, whether selfish or selfless, in self-transcendence. We manage to obscure the import of times of crisis and hide from ourselves the reality of death, so existence dwindles to a soft and comfortable continuum in which nothing sharply calls us to ourselves or calls us to account for what we are.

The truth that he who loves his life will lose it could scarcely be more obvious than in selfish attempts to affirm the self, no matter whether they are the desperate quests for security that bind the self to the everyday world and its accidents and uncertainties or else the random gratification of appetite that is encouraged by an affluent society where we need only stretch out a hand impatiently for whatever offers to satisfy the whims of the moment. The world always has its revenge, though, and grows tedious and enervating because it no longer affords challenges or occasions for struggle, no tests or times for momentous decision. So we stretch out our hands more often until desire becomes at the same time so wearied and so insatiable that it consumes even itself, leaving a trail of cold little habits of opened mouths and clenched fists and cold little fears that youth will someday disappear and the grip of the fingers will grow infirm. Desiring remains, a shadow of itself, but instead of an I that desires there is only a sort of empty sack, given its shape for the day by whatever happens to be thrown inside.

Intemperance is always blind. On the one hand, disinterested regard for the shape of reality is spoiled by the insistent clangor of one's own desires, and the self stands once again in the way of its vision; on the other, surrender to some of the hungers of the self that exclude others means that the range of vision is constricted. The few realities that sight can still recognize become more and more obsessive, and now the absolutizing instinct can flourish. Because the self is not its own master, vision becomes both more partial and more selfish. The eye of the mind dwells on a single fact or else flits from one to another in helpless submission to the whims of the individual, and the daimons bulk too large for a man to discover anything beyond them at all. So blindness brings boredom, for neither can vision encompass a sufficient range to satisfy the individual nor can it really see anything more than endless reflections of the self and its cravings. Boredom knows no way to escape from itself and ordinarily resigns itself to the hope that greater quantity will provide greater gratification; then

> it builds itself a world according to its own image and likeness . . . surrounds itself with the restlessness of a perpetual moving picture of meaningless shows, and with the literally deafening noise of impressions and sensations breathlessly rushing past the windows of the senses . . . a world which, to the piercing eye of the healthy mind untouched by its contagion, appears like the amusement quarter of a big city in the hard brightness of a winter morning: desperately bare, disconsolate, and ghostly.[3]

In the end, boredom turns away from the task of sight that selfishness has complicated and tries to find a remedy against itself in the pleasure of sight. Man no longer even wants to be a knower but is content to live as a voyeur.

Intemperance diminishes the responsiveness of the self to itself as well as to its world, and this sort of poverty is never a virtue but simply the death of love and the beginning of the love of death. On the other hand, selflessness and an excess of love for someone else can provoke a form of intemperance that has a certain nobility but that also conflicts directly with faith in God. Undialectical love for a child can betray us into intemperance and the loss of much of ourselves in the rash pursuit of what our children might require. We can no more purchase their security than we can assure our own, of course, but what we can do is either to instill our own intemperance in their expectations of instant gratification or else to cheat them of the freedom to risk and test themselves without which a child will never grow to be a man. Not only can we breed in them a reflection of our intemperance, not only are we unjust to the exigencies of our own self-affirmation because of the ways that we identify our fulfillment with the welfare of others, but our mistaken selflessness can also lay upon them a burden of gratitude that inhibits their proper self-affirmation. Even if we do not want the gratitude, the reasons for it and the impossibility of offering it are still there, eating away at the edges of awareness. Our selflessness can suffocate others as well as vitiate ourselves, growing intemperately until it becomes a sort of ontological insult, a violation of the richness of our own being. All the more important, then, is faith in a holy presence that sustains a realm of basic trust within which each person is freed from those who depend upon him as well as for them.

Temperance has a special relationship to faith, for there is no way to integrate the forces within the self apart from images of selfhood that faith affords. But if it is helpless without faith, the opposite is equally true; there can be no keeping of faith with the images of the self that faith provides if temperance is not present, too. In his fine study of the "cardinal" virtues, Pieper writes of the integral relationship between humor and humility, which recognizes that humanity is neither God nor even remotely like him in its estranged condition. The dependence of temperance upon faith is all the greater because of the importance of the unserious perception of human existence that revelation affords. In the light of the presence of God, none of man's appetites or projects or posturings is without its comic aspects; none must be regarded with unalloyed seriousness lest it begin to exclude others and grow to the stature of a *daimon*. The humor and humility that faith nurtures are our best instruments for shaping a perspective that can equip us to wrestle with what lies within ourselves, while the seriousness that blinds us to whatever is outside the range of our own selfish interests finds its principal ally, oddly enough, in the "funny." The differences between the comic and the funny are numerous and important.

When persons behave in unconventional ways, we tend to laugh because they seem funny to us. Our response serves a fundamental and quite legitimate social goal, which is the maintenance of the ways of the community, because laughter ordinarily forces the unconventional self back into the routinized patterns of behavior to which we have grown accustomed. But this little victory of the social world over the individual also discloses our fear of the stranger, and our laughter reflects a complacent sense of being different from him. We can afford to laugh because we are spectators, after all, watching a scene in which we are not involved and watching players who are, at least for the moment, strangers to us. Our perception of ourselves is not enriched, then, for we remain merely creatures of convention. Laughter may change the other self and so restore what has been normal and familiar, but unless we finish with our laughing the situation will do nothing to challenge our understanding of others or of ourselves. The funny is funniest because it happens to trap those who laugh in the "serious" world and reinforces their xenophobia.

The comic could not be more different, for it begins with a sense of the vulnerability and awkwardness and simple oddity of an individual and then discovers in this rude humanness some qualities that all men share. Suddenly our cherished illusions that we are unlike other men are punctured, and we are led to a new meeting with ourselves. Someone else slips on the proverbial banana skin, but so could we; despite all our pride and planning, our unique importance and lovableness, because of some cosmic oversight we are liable to the same ridiculous contingencies that surprise other people. Our most careful arrangements come unstuck in hopeless and lunatic ways for no good reason, and there bursts forth again the comedy of a creature who is not God but who constantly postures as though he were. The comic warns that every man could well be a participant and refuses to isolate the self from its brothers in the ways that the funny does. So the one nurtures individual humility, while the other fosters communal arrogance and contributes to alienation within society. One enforces homogeneity, while the other thrives on the recognition of the disparities, diversities, and incongruities by which our posturing is all undone. The funny tries to lead us away from the actuality of our humanness, but the comic calls us back again, stripping away illusions about the self and its powers to manage the world, healing vision that has been clouded by self-seriousness and self-concern. It rarely tells us much about the differences between ourselves and others, but states how very much we share. The comic impulse and the contemplative spirit are fruit of the same tree. The latter reflects upon the meaning of revelation and the former expresses it—the vanity of our pretensions, the relativity of our idols, the precariousness of the structures of meaning that we build for ourselves, and the utter oddity of the humanness that binds us together.

Temperance means order within the self, then; it describes the power to affirm the individual in all his wholeness and complexity. It is a form of justice that is directed toward all the potentialities and impulses within the self, so that men are freed from domination by what is either less or more than themselves. Because the individual is a creature of God, however, fashioned in such a way that he can find himself only in relation to God, temperance cannot complete its business apart from faith. Without it, temperance ends with the admonition, "In nothing too much," and so quantifies the problem of the quality and integrity of selfhood. Temperance needs faith, too, because mastery of the self depends upon images of selfhood; the attainment of every virtue finally becomes an affair of vision and perspective. Nothing will ever be achieved unless we are able to *see*.

Temperance is in even greater need of faith, however, because only the disclosure of the holy can illuminate the unseriousness of a world that always regards itself too seriously, and only the holy can provide a foundation for temperance on the certainty that there is no justification for any unqualified allegiance either to the lords of the earth or to the strange demands that eddy to and fro within the self. The root of all intemperance is simply our seriousness about ourselves, for this is what confirms our selfishness. The penalty exacted by our selfishness is that we become ever more serious about some elements within the self and lose touch with others, for our blindness to the true situation of man as a creature before God blinds us equally to some aspects of our humanness. If temperance can care for the individual alone, it is the sense of comedy that has brought him freedom and solitude where daimons used to roam. But the same sense of comedy also reminds us that our humanity is shared and shared richly by every other self, and so it undermines the barriers that we have carefully constructed in order to separate ourselves from strangers. It prepares us, therefore, to meet what justice demands.

Justice means *enabling the other to be his own master*.[4] It is concerned for the stranger, caring for rights that are inherently his as well as for the repayment of the indebtedness to him that we incur. It sanctions him in his separateness and affirms him in all of his otherness from ourselves. What justice must always recognize as his elemental and inalienable right is, quite simply, the opportunity to be able to become himself. His right to be and to do no less than this is not merely a fact that limits our own will to power, not merely something that we encounter in some adventitious way whenever we happen to wander outside familiar terrain. It approaches us and refuses to leave us untouched, invading our privacy and interrupting our times of relaxation. The rights and obligations that justice must acknowledge and support are there, antecedent to any contracts that we have decided to sign, prior to any agreements made within our society, older than any inheritance from ancestors whose promissory notes we must honor. The right to be one's own master must be affirmed and served wherever it confronts us for no other reason than this: the stranger is a *creature*.

God has willed the existence of this stranger just as much as the life of someone else who is a friend. God affirms him in his otherness from the divine and in his distinction from ourselves. God approves and sustains him, so Christians believe, not for the pleasure of the creator of the self but in order that this creature can reach out toward the sort of fulfillment appropriate to its own distinctive nature and actualize possibilities that no one else, not even the holy, could realize in quite the same way. The stranger is deserving, then, he has a *due*, because of a decision that comes from beyond the world of men, a decision that is completely beyond reversal or controversy or even discussion within society. This right of his reaches out and touches us simply because we are creatures, too, and our nature is fashioned for responsiveness to others. When we betray them, therefore, we have betrayed ourselves, disordering our nature so that we can no longer recognize our own rights or achieve all of our potentialities. This is what it means to speak of rights that are inalienable because they are the consequences of a decision by the source of life: when they are violated, the one who commits the violation becomes alienated from himself.

The antithesis of justice seems to be injustice, of course, but from a more theological perspective it appears to stand midway in the spectrum that runs from justice to indifference. Indifference allows others to do what they will; you can go your way and I will go mine, for there are no bonds between strangers unless they happen to move to the same neighborhood where the clash of interests means that strangeness will yield to enmity except for the uneasy alliances that are enforced by the presence of some new stranger on the streets. Writing of "one form of injustice that is extremely real," Pieper describes

> the kind of injustice that rests on man's having lost his contact with truth. To him the question as to whether a man has his due or not is absolutely and utterly irrelevant. As a result, something far more radically inhuman than formal injustice comes to the fore; for human actions are properly human because they have taken reality as their measure.[5]

Indifference is obviously the source of some of our failures to offer their due to others or to respect their rights. From a Christian point of view, however, indifference toward the stranger is even worse than the injustice it brings, for it means that the self has lost the truth of its own condition before God, its situation as a stranger who was embraced while ungodly, helpless, and an enemy. No longer can the Christian community begin to comprehend its own nature, for there can be no understanding apart from its confrontation with itself in the person of the alien and foreigner. Injustice is a failure to do the truth, an unwillingness to give the actual what is due to it. Indifference, though, does not even care for the truth; it has lost all appetite for actuality, and so it is the ultimate betrayal of that which is supremely actual. Injustice signifies the distortion of relationships, but indifference simply severs them. It forecloses possibilities that remain even in the most unjust of situations, and therefore it strikes at the heart of a creature who is made to find satisfaction only in relation to other selves and God. There are opportunities to argue in the name of justice against those who act unjustly, but indifference halts the conversation before it has a chance to begin.

Enabling the other to become his own master means far more than mere permission, much more than acknowledgment that the presence of the stranger imposes limits upon our own ambitions and desires. It involves an acceptance of responsibility and a commitment to the freedom of other persons. If a man is to become himself, our duty is to set him at liberty, freed from such dependence upon us and our charity that he is robbed of himself. Justice requires respect for and commitment to the strangeness of the alien, concern that he should be able to express all of his difference from the rest of us. If others are to find freedom, however, the principal aim of justice must be the provision of means rather than the distribution of ends; its real intention is not to do something for someone else but to afford him the opportunity to do something for himself. Justice is not committed to the provision of an equal amount of gratification for everyone, therefore, but to the realization of whatever measure of integrity and independence is possible for persons who are profoundly and always unequal. Its commitments are to actuality, not to the abstractions of mathematics, and it has no concern at all to give an equal share of everything to everyone. The question that it asks concerns how much this particular person needs in order to become his own master, defend himself in an unjust world, express the possibilities with which his nature is endowed. In every attempt to dispense or secure justice there is an element of self-interest, however, for we are unduly generous toward those who belong to our own communities and unduly mean toward those who do not. It is all the more important to emphasize, then, that for the sake of justice every person must be regarded as a stranger; whenever someone is admitted to a circle of familiars, inequity returns. But if we have been tutored within a community that finds its vocation in speaking with strangers, at least the danger will be lessened that the figure of the stranger will be the butt of our xenophobia instead of the creation of our passion for justice toward all.

To be a creature means that I am this single and singular self, not to be confused with anyone else, not to be replaced by anyone else, an individual who can realize possibilities that no other person has the opportunity to achieve at this particular time and place. On the other hand, it also means that I am one among many who share a common nature that draws us insistently toward others. I am dependent upon their speaking for my first intimations of transcendence, upon their imaginations for the expansion of my hope, upon their loving for a sense of the significance and worthiness of my own self. But if we are to love one another, we must have justice as well. Love will dwindle to a parody of itself and destroy whatever it seeks if justice is not at its side, affirming and guarding the otherness of whatever is loved. Love unites persons but justice preserves them in their union, lest one should become merely an extension of the other. On the other hand, it is equally true that there will not be justice apart from love. The reasons are many, but first among them is the fact that the ways we are loved teach us to respect and cherish ourselves so that we can affirm the rights of all the others who share our common humanness. Then, too, love aspires to community and reconciliation, but there can be no community without order, no reconciliation without the acknowledgment that order has been violated. As the ordering of our common life, justice is presupposed in what love desires; the ambition written into love motivates and sustains the concern to achieve justice.

It is true that love seeks union that will put an end to strangeness, while justice regards everyone as a stranger so that partiality toward some will not prevent recognition of the minimum due to all. Still, it is love in the form of imaginative sensitivity toward and careful scrutiny of some special others that provides the essential motive for regarding all persons as valuable and endowed with fundamental rights. It is a mistake to believe there is some single connection between love and justice; they are bound up in many ways, and this mutual dependence is no less evident in the relationship of justice to hope and faith. If our actions toward others reflect less than justice demands, not only have we deprived ourselves of reason to hope for their help but we have also disordered our own nature so that there is less reason to hope in ourselves. Nor are we then men of faith, for the absence of justice is sufficient proof that there are no longer images of man with the power to awaken the self to the meaning of its shared humanity. On the one hand, the theological virtues cannot survive if justice does not keep them company; on the other, justice cannot live in territory that has not already been possessed by faith, hope, and love. It requires faith in the inalienability of human rights because they have been established by a decision that cannot be disputed at this late hour, and hope that a world fashioned by a power committed to justice will prove amenable to the recognition of obligations and to the payment of debts.

In the world as we know it, we cannot pay all the debts that we incur or give to others all that is their due; we are always debtors, and therefore if justice is not consistently accompanied by love it will quickly become less than just. There are no ways to repay parents for the anguish that love has cost, or the God who has made us for the opportunity to be one's own self, or a forest for what it offers on a summer afternoon, or friends and sometimes even strangers for their unselfish acts of small sacrifice. A person who aspires to be just must also be much more; he must be grateful, too, for there is no other way to respond to what cannot ever be repaid. There are elements of grace in our common life, occasions when we are surprised by more than we could expect or ever deserve. Unfamiliar pleasures and gratuitous gestures of kindness stud the fabric of existence with a design of small marvels. While the mind busies itself with calculations of its indebtedness, the heart refuses to be satisfied with less than ungrudging responses that can give some expression to its gratitude toward others, toward the earth, and to God. The just man, as Pieper remarks, realizing

> that his very being is a gift, and that he is heavily indebted before God and man, is also the man willing to give where there is no strict obligation. He will be willing to give another man something no one can compel him to give. . . . The man who strives for justice, and he above all, realizes (Thomas says) that fulfilling an obligation and doing what he is really obliged to do are not all that is necessary. . . . Communal life will necessarily become inhuman if man's dues to men are determined by pure calculation. That the just man give to another what is *not* due to him is particularly important since injustice is the prevailing condition in our world. Because men must do without things that are due to them (since others are withholding them unjustly); since human need and want persist even though no specific person fails to fulfill his obligation, and even though no binding obligation can be construed for anyone; for these very reasons it is not "just and right" for the just man to restrict himself to rendering only what is strictly due.[6]

As an affair of mere calculation and recompense, then, justice is blind to what justice itself demands. Much of whatever we have was neither owed to us nor required by our rights. Gratitude is the form that justice must assume when it stands before gifts that cannot be repaid. It counsels that we should enable others to know the same abundance, even strangers, for nothing less is appropriate for someone who is always a fellow creature and potential thou, not merely the quotient of a million divided by a million. Justice reaches beyond itself once it has recognized a man's incalculable indebtedness before God, for then it can no longer busy itself simply with rights but is committed to treating as creditors other creatures to whom nothing is owed at all. In an unjust world, the needy demand more attention than the deserving. So justice must finally qualify its neutrality and adopt a consistent bias toward the vulnerable and defenseless, the widows and orphans, the twisted and handicapped, toward all those who need much in order to achieve for themselves the same modest fulfillment that others can attain with little aid. The next chapter will return to this problem.

Injustice avenges itself. That fact provides a poor motive for the pursuit of justice, poor at least beside the greater truth that the community for which love searches will dissolve without the order that justice brings. Nevertheless, the powerful can come to depend upon the helpless in more destructive ways than the poor depend upon the rich, for the master needs his slaves for the sake of his own definition of himself while the slaves are free to understand themselves without reference to their servitude. It is also true that the wretched of the earth whom indifference excludes have their particular ways to gain revenge. Their unfamiliar presence shadows the borders of awareness, threatening to violate the realm of the established and secure, spoiling the pleasures of a city walk. The gestures that would be baptized by familiarity now appear, in their suddenness, epiphanies of the daimonic and reasons for terror. Who are those people coming toward us so slowly in the dark? What is he holding in his hand? Why did he stop by our gate? Because he has not been enabled to become his own master, he is dangerous indeed. But fantasy begins to embroider his shadow, too, for early indifference is often penalized by later obsession. Instances of injustice or indifference become magnets, drawing up from the corridors of a sinful heart the filings of a thousand vague apprehensions and the ache of a loneliness we cannot cure. I am not free for others without temperance, and I am not free from others without justice.

On the other hand, justice is not only the cement that holds together foundations of society that injustice erodes. It is also subversive, challenging the shape of the present in the name of versions of equality not yet realized. What acts does justice require of us as compensation for injustices in which we have played no role? What judgment is justly shared by us because of what our neighbors have done while we kept silence? What gestures of penitence or sacrifice or protest are we now obligated to perform because we have not consistently employed our powers to work for social change before? The neutral perspective from which we thought that it would be possible to assess whether acts are just or unjust eventually betrays us, for there are mysteries about justice that only a wisdom higher than calculation will ever resolve. Sometimes we criticize the rough justice we have achieved in the name of more equal justice, but that notion is really a euphemism for something else. Love seeks communion in which strangeness is overcome. Justice seems different, because it insists that everyone is a stranger and then tries to affirm the alien in all the stubborn opacity of his strangeness. But if justice is to do so much, it must eventually recognize that it is just a synonym for *order within the goal of love.*

Courage means *mastery of the self in relation to others,* so that the greatest possibilities of selfhood can be realized. It holds a lower rank than justice, perhaps, which must instruct it in the causes for which sacrifice is the only humane resolve. It depends equally upon temperance, which tells it what justice toward the various elements within the self involves. The peculiarity of courage is that, like hope, there is always a "despite" set at the core of what it does. It knows how vulnerable men are and how frail a construction is the identity of the individual, but it musters the will and the power to affirm as much as possible of what the person might be, despite all the forces that conspire together against that affirmation and threaten to diminish or invade or enslave the self. Courage describes mastery in our relationships not only with other persons, however, but also to the contingent events that surprise us and the ineluctable realities of the human condition that no one can evade. The greatest of these, of course, is the reality of death. The cemetery in Northfield, Massachusetts, is much like a thousand others in New England, bordered on one side by the tracks of the Boston and Maine railroad and on another by the town dump. Many of the eighteenth-century gravestones are illegible now and vandalism has had its way with a few others, but among the inscriptions that can still be read on weathered slabs of slate are some that once were particularly common:

> Behold my grave as you pass by.
> As you are living, so was I.

Death Suddenly took hold of me,
And so the case with you may be.

Children and friends as you pass by
As you are now, so once was I.
As I am now, soon you will be.
Prepare for death and follow me.

Whilst young men
my tomb do view
Remember well
Here's room for you.

Beneath these clods of silent dust,
I sleep where all the living must;
The gayest youth and fairest face,
In time must bee in this dark place.

All courage refers to death, which frightens not because it is
unknown but because there are so many desolating epiphanies of
its presence in the everyday world. In every interrupted conversation, in every unheeded appeal, in every averted glance, in every
failure of comprehension, in whatever breakage reconciliation has
not healed, in all indifference and ingratitude, in loneliness and
enervation and illness, death is present even if not in fullness and
power. We are instructed in what it means to be an object, no
longer to be. On the one hand, courage finds small ways to struggle
against death, much as the figure of the matador in the writings of
Ernest Hemingway rehearses man's fate and achieves some penulti-
mate victory over it in a fashion that is intended to express whatever gracefulness and worth there is in our humanness. On the
other, courage learns to bear the pathos that accompanies mortality. Pathos is born in the movement from significance to insignificance. A child who has just lost his father, for example, watches
the garden that his father loved and the little shrubs that held such
significance for the man. Now their significance has passed to
insignificance. In his recognition of this passing, the child really
learns what the passing of his father means and grasps the pathos
of our common lot. Noel D. O'Donoghue writes:

We suffer when somebody dies whom we loved, but pathos
makes its appearance only when we turn up a letter and find in it
some characteristic turn of expression, brave and cheerful perhaps in face of pain or disappointment, or an old jacket, or a
pipe, or things arranged in a certain way in a bedroom or kitchen.
. . . For all his labour, for all his planning and striving, man
remains an alien, the victim of forces and processes beyond his
control; the home-light he carries within him is but a tiny candle-

flame in the immense surrounding darkness. The home-signifi-
cances he creates are always vanishing into the non-significance of
alienation. What opens out before him is the wide world of
pathos. And he is forced to ask himself whether it is along the
tearful roads of this world that the way to his true homeland
lies.[7]

Social experience can eviscerate courage just as much as it
can damage the other virtues and in just as many ways, but nothing else undermines the foundations of courage as rapidly as whatever obscures our mortality and dulls our eyes to what O'Donoghue
sees. The cosmetic impulse that opts for illusion instead of reality
cheats us of the opportunity to be ourselves, no matter whether
it is expressed in the advertising of the neighborhood druggist, the
official pronouncements on foreign affairs, or the unctuous whis-
pers of a friendly mortician. The disguise of the certainty of death
for every individual conspires with the pretensions to immortality
that arise from the social world and deprives the self of an independent existence even while it is alive. If this nation and culture
can elude hitherto universal rhythms of growth and decay, what
defenses do we have to guard ourselves from irremediable alienation within society? Then, too, the disguise blinds us to the
rhythms within ourselves and the inescapable movement from
youth to age; our understanding of ourselves is impoverished and
we go to our end unprepared. More important, we have lost the
motivation and denied ourselves the courage to struggle for the
remedy of interruptions and loneliness, and of indifference and
brokenness, because we have lost touch with the irrevocable reality that they intimate. Death is neither simply the end of life nor
a shadow that falls insistently upon it, though. The acknowledgment of mortality invests our lives with new urgency and richness,
for what can best free us from routine and convention, from the
incessant round of getting and spending, is simply the passionate
knowledge that I must die. Every morning death has edged a little
closer to my side.

While temperance and justice are well acquainted with the
truth that he who loves his life too much will lose it, courage is
prepared to act on that knowledge and risk life in order to find it.
In other words, it means the acceptance of insecurity because the
self is aware that security is finally an illusion in a world ruled by
death, where men are ever at the mercy of accidents and contin-

gencies and, not least of all, of their own enervation. Courage means that the self has learned to let things go, to release its grip upon the past in anticipation of what the future holds, to travel with little baggage so that the surprises of life will not catch it so encumbered that it cannot respond. Yet these are not courageous acts if the self does not understand the loss that it might incur or how greatly risk is compounded by its frailty. Like all the rest, the virtue of courage finally depends upon our ability to see. The extraordinary emphasis that Albert Camus gave to the importance of vigilance and lucidity was anchored in his knowledge that without them there can be no courage worth the name.

Courage injects an element of play into the most serious pursuits, testing the self for the simple pleasure of the challenge and courting tension for the joy of its resolution, secure in the knowledge that since life cannot be kept it is best spent in the best causes and most exhilarating games. Mastery of the self in relation to others demands surrender no less than victory, however, not only achievements but also offerings and reticences and sacrifices. So it must not be identified with agency, although this is a strong temptation in a culture as much oriented toward action and busyness as America. If courage is to affirm the wholeness of the individual, *anima* no less than *animus*, then it must involve the capacity to bear suffering as well as to alleviate it, to accept pain and death as well as to celebrate life, to yield before limits as well as to struggle against them, and to sleep as well as to watch through the night. The readiness to sacrifice and the acceptance of suffering are among the greatest works of courage, though perhaps the greatest of all is the resolve to look at the nature of the self in its entirety and admit the sickness there no less than the health. On that act of recognition depends all else that courage does. Sometimes it may have little power to banish the darkness that hangs over the heart or mind, but still the gesture of acknowledgment can provide at least some therapy and manage a partial disarmament of what it cannot completely exorcize.

Courage is twofold, affirming the self in its independence and in its belonging, as a whole in itself and as a part of greater wholes. Because we are what we are and nothing else at all, we are also a bewildering and wonderful variety—members of many communities, sources of many loves, ingested by many worlds, places where nature and history meet, intersections of past and future, tangles of what is and what might be and what has never been. But there would be no such variety if we were not just what we are, each quite individual and separate. Mysteriously enough, our identity becomes a far more rich and complex affair than could ever have been derived from the different relationships that first bestowed a sort of identity upon us. So courage always insists that the individual is more than a part of a whole, more than a part of many wholes, more than he has been given by all the communities and powers of the age, and that there is nothing he should be called to serve in a way that will condemn him to servitude.

Man's capacity to avoid the perils of anomie and alienation rests upon the dexterity with which the self can balance the two disparate ways that courage moves. If either were able to exclude the other entirely, then the self would lose its world or else be wholly lost within it, cannibalized by "they." Often one movement occurs at the expense of the other; greater participation jeopardizes independence or independence inhibits participation. In either instance, though, the self is no longer affirmed in its entirety, and therefore what is expressed has a daimonic vitality and ruthlessness about itself, an exaggerated strength that has soured because it is not at the service of complete selfhood. The strength that was intended to usher us to manhood has unmanned us because there is no longer a dialectical relationship between individuality and participation in which the strength of each heightens the vitality of the other. Instead, there is simply a neurotic display of energy in which we affirm ourselves in one way because we are deprived or afraid of another—as peers because we have failed as parents, as workers because we are scared of being alone, as strangers because once we were not invited to a party that we wanted to attend. The undialectical identity that we have purchased may be no less comforting because it is illusory, but it is a violation of our nature and costs us the creative insecurity that launches new ventures in the process of maturation.

Courage depends upon hope, for it can scarcely know what is demanded of it until hope explores the possibilities that the self can realize and discovers whatever help is at hand. What I will do depends upon what I can hope for, and hoping cannot afford to ignore the presence of others; what I must do, too, depends upon what others hope for from me. So courage is courageous enough to ask for assistance from the same communities and powers that threaten the self with captivity, and it is courageous enough not to desert its responsibilities there. Relatedness to what lies beyond the self is no less constitutive of our humanness than is relatedness to the self, and there are occasions when either can legitimately demand that we sacrifice even life itself, for only by that loss can we gain our lives or else retain unspoiled the life that we have known. But in the end, there is no reason for acts of such extraordinary courage unless we have more hope than simply the hope to acquit ourselves well. As Pieper observes, "To be brave means not only to suffer injury and death in the struggle for the realization of the good, but also to hope for victory. Without this hope, fortitude is impossible. And the higher this victory, the more certain the hope for it, the more man risks to gain it."[8] The greater the hope, the more willingness there is to accept the risk: the magnitude of courage is shaped by the expansiveness of our hope. If the self is grasped by the transcendent reality that is lord of death as well as lord of life, it can see beyond the certainty of its mortality that hitherto provided the ultimate motivation and challenge for courage. It can exhibit still greater daring, secured by the conviction that the whole world can be a realm of basic trust and is no longer an arid land where sacrifice is neither expected nor justified by its populace.

Courage is no less bound up with love and faith than it is with hope. After all, there is only a grotesque counterfeit of courage in the willingness to risk our lives if we do not believe that life itself is worthwhile. Courage is always a triumph over fear, unless men have failed to take the measure of their own frailty or of the power of the world, and there is no reason to fear the loss of anything we do not love. For what reason should we want to acquit ourselves well if the loving and caring of other people have not tutored us to enjoy the self and persuaded us to cherish what we are? How can we cherish ourselves, though, if we have no splendid images of what selfhood means? How can we manage any affirmation of the self if we have no faith that bestows powerful images, if we have no faith in the images that call us to the keeping of faith, if we have no faith in a reality by which we are called to the keeping of faith? What motive is there to face the "despite" that courage involves if we have no faith in the agency of the self, no hope of success, no love for what we struggle to express? Again, it is true that behind all else, shaping our vision and gaining from it their shape: faith, hope, love abide, these three.

8
playing fair

Unlike the virtues that are sometimes called "theological," temperance and justice and courage do not differ in their nature but only in their focus. Temperance resolves that justice must be done to all the powers and possibilities of the self. Because it is concerned with justice for the sake of the wholeness of the person, it is not unfamiliar with the sacrifices that must often be demanded of what is less than the whole. But if it subordinates the parts to the whole, it is equally concerned that none of them should be vitiated or excluded simply because of the greediness of others. Courage commits itself to justice toward all the possibilities of the self in its transactions with other persons, but it also becomes ever better acquainted with the magnitude of the sacrifices that are sometimes required of a creature who must lose his life in order to find all the possibilities that life enshrines. Justice concerns itself with the integrity and rights of other selves, and it is prepared to honor the demands for sacrifice that are levied not only in the name of what is due to others but also for the sake of some expression of gratitude for all the gifts that the self did not deserve and cannot ever repay. Temperance is busy with the lands inside the self, courage with the acreage in the world that a man must cultivate for himself, and justice with the domains of others. But the three are really one in the sense that they share a single commitment to justice or *fair play*, to being fair and playing fair with all that lies outside the self and all the terrain that lies within. Justice must be more than just if it is ever to be entirely just within a fallen world, however, or so it is instructed by the advent of the holy. But if we are to recognize that presence when it draws close to us, we must be schooled in still another virtue, the virtue of prudence.

On the one hand, temperance and justice and courage are the only indexes we have of whether the self has appropriated the gifts that it has received from others—our experiences of being loved and gently shoved toward liberation, the judgments upon our lying and the occasions when we were comforted for a bruised knee or because of our fear of the night, our times of being trusted and empowered to trust and to hope in and with other people. Temperance means the actualization of some of the images of self-hood that our faiths provide; it does not come before faith but does a little better and practices it. Faith without temperance indicates that the imagery provided by faith no longer exacts our trust and loyalty. Courage achieves the realization of possibilities that hope discerned but could not hope to actualize without the hope of courage. Justice guards the opportunity for love to grow into a mature and mutual affair instead of the dependent relationship that childhood or sickness involves; neither less than love nor a substitute for it, justice is one side of the goal at which love aims.

So the "natural" virtues express the maturation of the self, enabling love to realize its ambition, hope to find the strength it needs, faith to keep faith. These are the three ingredients of being free and becoming a law unto oneself under God: mastery of the self, mastery of the self in relation to others, and enabling others to be their own masters as well. On the other hand, they are achievements that the self cannot create ex nihilo, as though it were a god, but only from the resources that it has been given. Temperance depends upon faith for its images, and faith upon experiences of the trustworthiness of the world and of other selves that a person can scarcely offer to himself. Justice depends upon love for its motive, and the capacity for love that is more than mere desire is a dividend born from all the variegated childhood receipts of the love and caring of others. Courage depends upon hope for its sustenance, and the magnitude and realism of hope are contingent upon all the others on whom one can count and in whom one can trust not only for some momentary aid but for an expansiveness of imagination that can complement and cure one's own. Temperance and justice and courage begin together and depend upon one another because they are committed to the same end, the goal of fair play. But there is only a single place where they can find room to grow, and that is where faith and hope and love have been before them and tilled the soil.

When faith or hope is approached from a Christian perspective and regarded as an "effect of grace," a response to the disclosure of God come among men and active on their behalf, then the greatest lesson taught by explorations of the notion of virtue is that grace never warps or truncates the integrity of the self but affirms and restores it. Without grace, there is no achievement of maturity or possibility of autonomy, because everything else depends upon the presence of faith, hope, and love. Without autonomy, grace has not achieved its goal, for the possibilities that it affords have not been grasped and actualized by the self. Grace does not trespass upon the boundaries of freedom but expands its province, for only through the mediation of grace by such humble acts as a moment of admiration for the color of a child's new pair of shoes can we enable the small self to establish its identity and learn to exercise its agency. What is true of our most elementary and common experience can be no less true in the meetings of the human with the holy. When grace is acknowledged to describe the presence of the father of all, it neither fosters some new sort of dependence nor reaffirms the old. Instead, imagination is kindled so that the individual can realize more of his potentialities because, at least as the Christian community understands the affair, in the concatenation of myths and stories lodged in this tradition there are more challenging and expansive images of what autonomous selfhood means than can ever be found in cities that are allegedly secular.

Sometimes in human affairs, the external wars against the internal, society against the individual, our undialectical faiths and loves against the self that entertains them. But this cannot occur in the transactions of men with their own source and sustainer. Grace, or what is outside the individual, communicates to what is inside the necessary resources for the expression of that interiority in some new and freer fashion. Every examination of the meaning of virtue must return again and again to acknowledge the dependence of freedom upon grace, of achievements upon gifts, of the internal upon the external, and autonomy upon what others have done. As with parent and child, so with God and man: the aim of grace is to enable the immature to become adult. The obverse of that, of course, is equally true. As with parent and child, and so with the holy and the human, no father can be a man for his son. In our dependence, in our betrayals by others, in the random violence suffered by what we value, we will never find a way to give sufficient account for our own coarseness of speech, for our bruised conscience, for our inabilities to honor the trusting of others. Grace does not free us from the self but calls us toward it, and there we are set new and arduous tasks.

Within the Christian tradition there has long been a common convention that has had misleading consequences, even though it has not been observed everywhere, always, or by all. People have believed that they could distinguish between two sorts of virtue, one of which is "natural" because they can attain it by their own efforts while the other is "theological," despite its natural analogues, because at least in its Christian form it depends entirely upon the grace of God. But every chapter of this essay has added its own bit of evidence that the distinction should be abandoned; it is not faithful to our experience, the clarity it promises to offer is spurious, and it twists and distorts whatever truth there is in the traditional polarity of nature and grace. The first of the arguments that we have seen against it is simply that faith and hope and love are not always theological, even by implication, but just thoroughly human affairs that are mediated to the individual through every one of his significant relationships. Apart from the images furnished by these relationships, we have no resources to construct our sense of identity as members of the commonwealth of man.

A second argument is that faith and hope and love are never purely theological, but even when inspired by the disclosure of the holy are still entangled with other versions of themselves, sometimes judging and qualifying lesser loyalties, sometimes reaffirming their significance, but never untainted by them and finally bereft of any relationship to them at all. Sometimes our multifoliate varieties of common trust and loyalty point beyond themselves and lead to more expansive faiths, and sometimes our most expansive and selfless commitments suddenly disclose their anchorage in the cellars of the mind, where they live with a welter of unworthy fears and small vanities that can be exorcized only by a time of crisis when selfish hopes find no answer but are themselves thrust into question by events beyond our control, the reversal suggesting new answers that transcend any of which we might have dreamed. Faith in the holy always betrays its earthly connections just as surely as, for those who believe, common sorts of loyalty and trust intimate the grace of God.

At one and the same time, then, the realm of the natural provides our last defense against and only means of access to the presence of the holy. The orientation of every sort of virtue is the same, toward the density and depth of the realm of the actual; some brands of faith stop with the finite and definite, and others grasp the ingredients of this world in their relationship to God, but there are no meetings with the holy apart from the mediation of the temporal and spatial realities of the earth. Were it not for the analogies as well as the conflicts among our different faiths and loves, it would be difficult to recognize the meaning of Christian discourse and to present Christian commitment as a significant option. The distinction between natural and theological tends to exalt Christian forms of faith, hope, and love as though they were neither subverted nor reinforced by earthly commitments. So we fail to acknowledge either the magnitude of our indebtedness to common life or the ease with which the virtues shrink to similitudes of themselves within Christian community, where often they mask lesser loyalties, narrow prejudices, selfish perspectives, and greedy quests for security. The distinction does nothing to sharpen the perspective of the church upon itself as a community of sinners and a sinful community—and, after all, only God knows what it means to speak of "saving faith." We might leave complicated distinctions in his hands.

The conventional procedure, then, does nothing to honor faith, hope, and love but achieves exactly the contrary, diminishing their significance because it obscures their importance for the cultivation of all other virtues. In fact, they are not some late and supranatural addition to the self but the one foundation without which there can be neither temperance nor justice nor courage. So the "natural" virtues might well be called theological and recognized as effects of grace, for they depend entirely upon the presence of faith, hope, love, and the gifts from others that preside at the latter's birth. In the same way, the "theological" virtues deserve to be called natural because in one form or another they are present wherever there is health; they are presupposed, whether recognized or not, in every struggle to gain the autonomy of the self. The holy wrestles with them and works within them so that they might expand to embrace all that is actual, but they are volatile affairs, refusing to remain what they were and always moving in one direction and then another. In the anomaly that the distinction between natural and theological can be stood on its head with equal or even greater plausibility, there is more evidence that contemporary Christian reflection can find little honest nourishment in all the conventional polarities between the religious and the secular, the saving and the common, or the sacred and the profane.[1] There is so much quicksilver in the metal of our life together that the stuff of it cannot be hammered into conformity with patterns as static and inflexible as these. The holy and the human are all that matter, and they are enough.

A final argument against attempts to differentiate between natural and theological is that they eventually separate what they try to distinguish. When faiths gain some theological resonance, as well as when they do not, there is all the difference in the world between one version that offers a greater measure of liberty and another that enforces alienation into functions and roles. Their different capacities to nurture the "natural" virtues provide ways to discriminate between the better and the worse. Temperance, justice, and courage, then, have some normative significance for the weighing and testing of our faiths; their health provides or else withholds a certain measure of existential validation. Far from subordinate to faith because they are merely "natural" while it is "theological," in fact they constitute the court before which it must plead its case.

The separation, therefore, deprives a Christian natural theology of one of its important tasks. Because loyalty and trust are not always goods, while justice is a good forever, it is necessary to assess their quality in its terms. Because different varieties of faith, hope, and love sometimes conflict and sometimes offer one another mutual support, it is wise to study their entanglements from the perspective of justice as fair play. Because daimons emerge when faith, hope, and love are divested of their dialectical character, it is important to stress their perverse theological dimension. At least to the eyes of faith, the "theological" virtues are often no less theological when they are unaware of the religious potential written into themselves, for they always testify in one way or another to the ecstatic impulse in man and to the ways it can lead him to the loss of the self, even though it is also the finest attribute of his essential nature. But these are responsibilities that can scarcely be fulfilled if we sever "natural" and "theological" or if faith, hope, and love are themselves separated into two camps, one strictly Christian and theological and immaculate while, far beneath it, there live some humble natural analogues that require no theological scrutiny.

Temperance, justice, and courage all counsel fair play; therefore, it is important to clarify the fundamental principles that regulate the expression of fairness in the different individual virtues. They can be derived in different ways, of course, and in *A Theory of Justice* John Rawls does this from the perspective of a contractual understanding of human community. The first concern of justice is with the basic structure of society that determines distribution of the primary goods that everyone wants. If the principles that shape and inform this structure are just, they will be ones at which common consent would arrive if we were to accept the hypothesis of an original situation or "state of nature" in which no one were aware of his natural or social advantages in relation to some persons and his disadvantages in relation to others. According to Rawls, the propriety of the idea of "justice as fairness" depends upon the hypothesis of an original situation in which agreements are fair because all parties are equally ignorant of their natural endowments and social circumstances. The principles of justice to which they agree are those that "free and rational persons concerned to further their own interests would accept in an initial position of equality as defining the fundamental terms of their association."[2]

When ignorance of the particularities of the situation of the individual precludes every quest for privileged position in the task of definition, reason dictates the choice of two principles that must be acknowledged everywhere and always. On the one hand, there must be equality in the distribution of basic rights and duties; on the other, the inequalities that nature legislates or that are the legacies of history and circumstances can be regarded as just only insofar as they serve the welfare of all the members of the community, and the interests of the least advantaged no less than the advancement of the individuals whom they most favor.[3] The initial imprecision in the argument that inequalities should be "to everyone's advantage" and related to positions that are equally open and equally "open to all"[4] Rawls eventually reformulates in this statement of the twin principles on which just or fair society is predicated:

First Principle
Each person is to have an equal right to the most extensive total system of equal basic liberties compatible with a similar system of liberty for all.

Priority Rule
The principles of justice are to be ranked in lexical order and therefore liberty can be restricted only for the sake of liberty. There are two cases: (a) a less extensive liberty must strengthen the total system of liberty shared by all, and (b) a less than equal liberty must be acceptable to those citizens with the lesser liberty.[5]

Second Principle
Social and economic inequalities are to be arranged so that they are both (a) to the greatest benefit of the least advantaged and (b) attached to offices and positions open to all under conditions of fair equality of opportunity.[6]

Fairness means that the favored are permitted to benefit only in ways that maximally serve to improve the condition of the persons who have lost. This is the dictate of the "difference principle," the strongly egalitarian rule that an equal distribution is to be preferred unless some different distribution will bring even greater improvement to the situation of both parties.[7] The principle does not involve an objection to inequality as such, which would be futile, but simply insists that inequality must serve not only a few persons, nor even many at the expense of a few, but every member of the community. Therefore, it represents a compact to understand "the distribution of natural talents as a common asset and to share in the benefits of this distribution whatever it turns out to be. . . . In justice as fairness men agree to share one another's fate."[8] In other words, in the common ignorance that characterizes their original "state of nature," it is rational for men to agree upon some version of the principle of redress. Undeserved inequalities deserve compensation, and so those who are socially, economically, or by nature disadvantaged require greater attention than those who are not if all persons, indeed, are to receive even a rough approximation of equal treatment from the totality of forces that shape their different destinies.

Fairness suggests that the entire commonwealth of man is best understood by analogy to its primary agency of socialization, the family, because especially within this context persons refrain from exploiting natural and social contingencies for selfish purposes and use them, instead, only for a greater measure of common good. The idea, Rawls writes, is that

> of not wanting to have greater advantages unless this is to the benefit of others who are less well off. The family, in its ideal conception and often in practice, is one place where the principle of maximizing the sum of advantages is rejected. Members of a family commonly do not wish to gain unless they can do so in ways that further the interests of the rest. Now wanting to act on the difference principle has precisely this consequence. Those better circumstanced are willing to have their greater advantages only under a scheme in which this works out for the benefit of the less fortunate.[9]

Fairness requires many different perspectives upon the social order, and so it is necessary to specify a variety of representative individuals. They are scarcely neutral observers, of course; neither are we, for rational self-interest dictates the point of view of everyone. Precisely for that reason, no perspective is so important as that of the least advantaged. Because these are powerless, systematic provisions for their consistent inclusion must be made by the powerful.

The voice of those who are deprived is the one we are most reluctant to hear, their vision the one we are most unwilling to entertain. Yet there is no certain way to assess whether the higher expectations of some people are just unless the wretched of the earth have their own equal vote in deciding whether those anticipations really "work as part of a scheme which improves the expectations of the least advantaged."[10] Although Rawls himself does not refer to strangers, they provide the paradigm of the least advantaged, for even the poorest insider does not suffer the discrimination levied against the outsider. But the stranger brings a perspective that is unfamiliar not only to those who are favored; it is alien to the social order as a whole, challenging common conceptions and preoccupations, exploring new opportunities for fairness to which familiarity is blind. So familial imagery needs to be complemented by the figure of the stranger, the one whom, like God, xenophobia tries to lock outside the city walls. When it is faithful to its vocation of speaking with strangers, the church can offer its own signal contribution to the maintenance of what the principles of justice require.

A particularly significant element in Rawls's argument is the claim that the primary social goods include not only liberty, wealth, and income but that among them "self-respect has a central place."[11] Although his appeal is not a prudential one, he recognizes that those who cannot respect themselves will not learn to respect others and that contempt for the self will always expand to touch other persons and erode the bonds of community. He argues that justice as fairness supports a sense of the worth of the self more than do other interpretations of social rights and duties and that this affords a persuasive reason to accept it. When the basic order of society is shaped by the two principles of fairness, the good of everyone

> is included in a scheme of mutual benefit and this public affirmation in institutions of each man's endeavors supports man's self-esteem. The establishment of equal liberty and the operation of the difference principle are bound to have this effect. . . . By arranging inequalities for reciprocal advantage and by abstaining from the exploitation of the contingencies of nature and social circumstance within a framework of equal liberty, persons express their respect for one another in the very constitution of their society. In this way they insure their self-esteem as it is rational for them to do.[12]

Rawls understands all obligations that the individual incurs in terms of the principle of fairness, which counsels that the self ought to do its part in accordance with the rules of a game or institution, at least when these rules and institutions do not depart from the fundamental principles of justice. If they are unjust no obligations arise, because the parties in the original situation when the social contract was articulated would not agree to the idea of unjust obligations. The features that distinguish obligations from "natural duties" are three. They are consequences of voluntary acts: we accept or offer promises or at least position ourselves so that some benefits accrue to us. Their content is defined by institutions or by socially accepted rules that specify what we are obliged to do. Finally, they are owed to some specific individuals who are engaged with us to maintain and benefit from a particular social arrangement. Unless we accept benefits or else employ some opportunities that institutions provide in order to further our own individual interests, no obligations arise.[13] The main idea, as Rawls sees it,

> is that when a number of persons engage in a mutually advantageous cooperative venture according to rules, and thus restrict their liberty in ways necessary to yield advantages for all, those who have submitted to these restrictions have a right to a similar acquiescence on the part of those who have benefitted from their submission. We are not to gain from the cooperative labors of others without doing our fair share. The two principles of justice define what is a fair share in the case of institutions belonging to the basic structure.[14]

The obligations that fairness calls us to honor, however, can also be understood as instances in which we voluntarily enlarge the compass of our natural duties. Because "a fundamental natural duty is the duty of justice," it follows that if the structure of society is just "everyone has a natural duty to do his part in the existing scheme. Each is bound to these institutions independent of his voluntary acts, performative or otherwise."[15] If we then voluntarily accept the benefits or opportunities that some institutions afford and incur obligations to them, we place ourselves within a sphere where their rules are doubly pertinent and we are bound by the natural duty of justice to honor those rules. On the other hand, Rawls prefers to retain the distinction between obligations and natural duties in order to emphasize how obligations freely undertaken can reinforce and deepen the dictates of natural duties, and "to emphasize the manner in which many ties are freely assumed, it is useful to have the principle of fairness."[16]

The Christian vision must affirm and include the principle of fairness. If it does not quarrel with the content awarded to the principle in *A Theory of Justice*, however, there still exist very important differences between the story of a social contract and the story of a divine covenant. For Rawls, fairness is an appropriate category because of its reference to the fiction of an original situation so characterized that rational agreements emerging from it must be fair to all parties. For Christian faith, fairness is an appropriate principle because it refers to an "original" situation meant to structure all commerce among men and fair because it represents the will of God. God wills and affirms the creature, creates and sustains a realm for the expansion of creaturely freedom, guards and restores it not for his own sake but entirely for the good of man. The will of God is the supreme instance and paradigm of the way that justice lies within and orders love, for this love seeks separation as well as union, difference as much as communion. God deals fairly with his creature and by a decision from beyond the human affirms that justice is always due, every man's right, the duty of all.

It is the creatureliness shared by all men that irrevocably commits them to the duty to share one another's fate, to regard natural talents as assets held in common, to affirm the cruciality of the difference principle, to affirm the stranger as a significant other, to embrace the principle of redress, to interpret the whole human community by means of the familial imagery that also enables man to address his lord. Neither in Rawls's version of social contract nor in Christian theology are principles of justice derived from a sense of man's inherent worth and dignity, but from a source that establishes worth where it is otherwise questionable and affirms dignity where it is otherwise never beyond dispute. There is also a difference, of course, for Rawls relies upon principles that are affirmed as universally valid by autonomous individuals while, for the eyes of faith, the inalienable worth of persons derives from the will of a power that is more than human. Consequently, the notion of gratitude has a far greater role to play in a Christian interpretation of fairness than in any variety of contract theory, and it is especially the virtue of prudence that provides the reasons for living gratefully.

For Rawls, as we have said, all obligations can be interpreted plausibly as voluntary extensions of the idea of natural duty. From a theological perspective, however, it might be appropriate to argue the reverse, for there is a sense in which gratitude counsels that all natural duties should be voluntarily affirmed as obligations. After all, in the very act of existence all men freely accept benefits from the author of life and so incur obligations not only to him but to all that he sustains. However we may specify the different natural duties, at least they are incumbent upon us quite apart from the ways that we have used our freedom and they are owed not only to some persons but to all who claim to be human. They are not dependent upon social practices or our relationships to various institutions but apply everywhere, always, and to all.[17] Natural duties reflect the will of him to whom all are incalculably indebted, indebted for their liberties, indebted for their lives. There is no way to repay the author of the gift of life except by gratitude. An appropriate expression of gratitude is the voluntary reaffirmation of natural duties as obligations that the self wills to entertain for the sake of him who seeks fair play and appropriate creaturely fulfillment for everything that he has made. Rawls notes that the obligations imposed by the principle of fairness "can support a tie already present that derives from the natural duty of justice."[18] When it is extended in the name of gratitude to cover the natural duties that individuals owe to one another, the idea of obligation can expand and enrich their meaning, suggesting acts of sacrifice and supererogation that the natural duties themselves never demand.

A Theory of Justice is concerned primarily with principles that can govern the fundamental constitution of society and secondarily with the relationships of individuals to the institutions from which they benefit. But there are theological reasons to extend the principle of fairness to include situations where there seems to be no strict obligation—and particularly to the transactions of individuals with one another and with themselves, as the exigencies of their life together are expressed in the virtues of temperance, justice, and courage. In the argument of this essay, however, "fair" is used to qualify the idea of playing and to invest with greater content the image of man as player. For the man who understands himself as a player, a fair player, the idea of obligation is expanded indefinitely; always there is an element of freedom in the game of life, everywhere there now are certain rules, and the particular persons to whom he is obligated become all people.

The problem remains, though, that persons must be provisioned to heed the principles of fairness and to respond to the injunctions of temperance, justice, and courage. How is someone to learn to see himself as a man who plays fairly or to envision his life as a game with rules by which he must abide? How can a person finally justify such a perception of himself when justice and courage demand sacrifices that can have weird and terrible consequences in a contingent world where deeds are rewarded in ways that no one could anticipate and where accident is often and coarsely king? These questions bring us back to the argument that actions depend upon vision, vision upon images, images of the self upon relationships to what lies beyond the self. They bring us back, too, to acknowledge the involution of faith and temperance, hope and courage, love and justice, and the theological and the natural, because the most secure and incontrovertible justification for the image of man that supports the idea of fair play is the disclosure of the holy. There are other ways to justify fair play, of course, and most often it is practiced without lengthy reflection or particular concern for reasons that will support the practice. But at least there are specifically Christian reasons to insist upon the integral relationship among all the virtues. Faith and its companions discover a story that provides man with the master image of the player; then temperance, justice, and courage tutor man in its moral significance so that it can be not only a theological image but a reality that informs and redresses the inequalities of our common life.

One of the arguments of *Grace and Common Life* is that a comic perception of self and society is an implicate of the revelation of God. The disclosure of the holy endows existence with a strange mixture of seriousness and unseriousness that it did not hitherto possess, first of all because now self and society are both displaced from the center of things and the comedy of their pretensions is exposed. Man is liberated from the fearful burden of belief that he alone is responsible for the world's destiny or that there is no court of appeal beyond the contemporary social order. Now he is free to close his eyes for a moment, to forget a few conventions, to dream, to play; at last he is a guest in the world and can afford to ignore some of the cares once enforced upon him by the illusion that he was its proprietor. On the other hand, the presence of God also means that man is called to radical accountability, radical in the sense that now he is responsible not only for his choices but for the choice of a self that chooses in this fashion. He is called to account not only for what still lies within his realm of possibilities but for the loss of all the unexplored possibilities of which his earlier decisions have deprived him.

There is an element of comedy in the contradiction between his accountability and what actually lies within his power, and this man who by his own hand has become so woefully made and finely abused stands helpless before it. There seems to be no particular relationship between the comic impulse and playing, which is often profoundly serious, because the one thrives on the violation of expectations while the other depends upon the maintenance of rules. Nevertheless, both mean liberation from the sort of deadly seriousness about the self that conflicts irremediably with faith in God. By means of the image of the player, man can best acknowledge the disparity between his apparent situation within the world and the subversion of all worldly claims, customs, and authorities by the address of a power that transcends the world and calls man to its service, thereby qualifying every finite relationship as well as the relation of the self to itself.[19]

Sometimes the principles we hold seem unrelated to the stories that inform our culture and constitute our heritage, and which have been told to us in a thousand forms since we were very small. But the principles have actually been derived from the stories, and their power to claim us depends upon the efficacy with which they remind us of their provenance. Persons decide that they will act as Christians, in other words, because they find themselves grasped by and held within the narrative of Jesus Christ; their principles are signs, tokens, and reminiscences of this story and of their identification with it. Our different modes of conduct, then, finally are shaped by the different stories that have captured our different selves. These provide us with the worlds within which we can see, with the narratives that enable us to model the diversity of our lives into a narrative form that displays some coherence and consistency. Principles are important because stories can be misinterpreted; their concrete moral significance is not apparent to casual inspection. Stories are important because principles can be applied in disastrous ways, and rules are often impotent to move us if we have not been ingested by the world of the story they represent and call us to reiterate.[20]

Moral life depends upon vision, but vision is unanchored and purposeless unless sight serves the sort of consistency and coherence that we describe by the idea of character. Character means that we are more or less rational narratives, and its achievement depends upon the narratives that we have heard or seen and somehow managed to make our own. Our social history and individual situation provide us with many stories and fragments of stories, however, with many images of what it means to be a man and many metaphors that disclose something of the world. If we are to become one self instead of many, an agent and not merely a patient, a unity rather than an accident of our history, then some of these images and narratives must be affirmed as dominant, crucial, always deserving loyalty, superior to all others, and intended to qualify them in ways that serve the interest of whatever story is regarded as primary. The connection between principles and stories has often been noted, but it is equally important to recognize that between the rule and the narrative, between the abstraction and the earthy story where it was born, there lives the image. Every significant narrative contains images many and various, of course, but among them there are never many that can serve as *master* images, enabling us to grasp concretely and practically what the story means. A master image provides a distillation of a story; among several options, the best is the one that enshrines the most possibilities for articulation of the entire narrative.

Master images must not be confused with world views, and for a variety of reasons. First, they are as richly metaphorical as the stories that they express, and in this multidimensionality lies their difference from principles. Second, they are more directly concerned with the self than with its world, with the perspective from which we see rather than with its consequences for what we see. Indeed, they are master images because they address the most fundamental aspect of vision, the problem of perspective. Unlike world views, too, they must possess a sort of indeterminacy that precludes either inflexible moral policies or confining orthodoxies in the interpretation of the meaning of life, precisely because their significance as master images resides in the richness and diversity that they afford for the articulation of the whole story from which they come. They are not intended to minimize the significance of other imagery drawn from the same narrative; on the contrary, they are meant to render it all the more intelligible and important because of the ways that they qualify and integrate and illuminate the rest. Obviously enough, if master images are not themselves qualified and enriched by all the other metaphors in the story, they are not master images at all. The more numerous are the images of the self as moral agent that a narrative provides, the more numerous will be the possibilities for individual life, because we do not intend what we cannot see and image ourselves accomplishing. Even so, there still must be a master image that expresses the unity within the variety and that condenses the sprawl and prosody of the narrative into a concrete and powerful metaphor which is able to acquaint the self with the core of whatever the story means.

The image of the player can most satisfactorily express the

anthropology of the Christian story and represent a Christian view of the situation of the self before God and in relation to its own self, other selves, and the powers of the world. On the other hand, the play impulse is as deeply written into other animals as it is imbedded in man, and, as every child knows, the interpretation of the self as a player and of life as a game can be derived from many sources apart from revelation. Some forms of play seem to know few rules that men must obey, and others encourage all sorts of aggressiveness and exclusiveness, displaying their parentage in feelings of anomie or alienation from the fabric of home or society. So the image of the player must be scrutinized consistently from the perspective of the universally applicable principle of fairness. A Christian image of man must affirm and include what the principle teaches and acknowledge that the dictates of temperance, justice, and courage afford a normative point of vantage from which to assess different versions of what playing involves.

The relationship between principle and image is internal and organic. There can be no genuine play without rules that are fair to everyone, or so the principle insists. There can be no life in accordance with the principle, unless there is an image of man that binds him to those rules. Playing fair is a style of life that is subject to constant jeopardy, however, not only because we are willing and eager to compromise our commitments to fairness but even more because it is so difficult to envision the self as a player if its world is not somehow transformed into a realm of basic trust. No one can play with consistency or joy if he dwells forever in the valley of the shadow of death, not even children who do not know how long the valley or notice how deep the shadow. But there is at least as much in our world to challenge basic trust as there is to confirm it. How can faith in such a realm be sustained by what is less than God? How can faith in God be sustained amidst the world as we know it? If answers to those questions always elude consensus, at least most of us agree to tailor our worlds, no matter how universal may be the commitments of which we boast, and so we content ourselves with a little clearing in the forest where it is relatively safe to play fair.

Still, it is not irrelevant to ask whether or in what senses the story embodied by the master image is true. It is true in the sense that it is descriptively true to the principle of fairness that rational creatures must affirm if they are to be moral selves. It is also descriptively true in the sense that it is true to the meaning of selfhood; in other words, it provides the necessary resources so that the self can achieve consistency and coherence, a fundamental direction for itself or individual character. Then, too, it is open to the sort of verification that I. T. Ramsey describes when he writes of the "method of empirical fit." In his comparison of the older "picture" models and the more recent "disclosure" models of man and the world that have led to increased knowledge in the arts and sciences, Ramsey locates the source of the latter in "a universe that discloses itself to us in a moment of disclosure."[21] There must be something, he continues,

> about the universe and man's experience in it which, for example, matches the behavior of a loving father. . . . In other words, we have a particular doctrine which, like a preferred and selected shoe, starts by appearing to meet our empirical needs. But on closer fitting to the phenomena the shoe may pinch. When tested against future slush and rain it may be proven to be not altogether watertight or it may be comfortable—yet it must not be, too comfortable. In this way, the test of a shoe is measured by its ability to match a wide range of phenomena, by its overall success in meeting a variety of needs. Here is what I might call the method of empirical fit.[22]

Whether the image of the player meets a variety of needs without betraying the story it is intended to express cannot be decided, of course, except by the exploration of what lies within the image. No matter how inclusive it is, there always remains a need for complementary images, for the figures of the stranger, the voyager, the son and brother and penitent. But it is important to recognize that playing fair is not only an implicit affirmation of grounds for basic trust, it also contributes to the preservation and expansion of such a realm, thereby providing its own small measure of verification for self and others that this is, indeed, God's world. Furthermore, the individual who perceives himself by means of the image of the player expects fairness not only in what he does but equally in what is done to him. The expectation is unjustified, for there is no persuasive evidence that this is a moral universe. But the simple willingness to question whether whatever is visited upon the self might not be fair can lead us away from our self-absorption and self-righteousness, remind us that we are judged as well as judges, recall the significance of stories of penitence and sacrifice, and so rekindle rather than dampen our commitments to playing fair. The individual who grasps himself as a player, then, can affirm and extend the realm of basic trust that faith in God descries, and he can do this by his interpretation of what he suffers as well as by what he does.

In *Grace and Common Life*, the merit of the image of the player is discussed in terms of the way that it manages to knit together moral and theological concerns within a Christian perspective. Playing is the strongest possible affirmation of the self apart from its functions and roles and everydayness; it is a remedy for alienation within society, but its emphasis upon rules also protects us from anomie. Play is the first child of the imagination, and the more complex its form the more profound is its vindication of imagination as the architect of selfhood. As it spins whole galaxies of new worlds, so can imagination furnish endless new visions of what it means to be a self, luring the individual to the pursuit of new options, calling him to new ways to realize possibilities that were never even recognized in the realm of the everyday, reminding him that still the I transcends every imaginative vision of itself. Playing vindicates the agency of the self, telling of the importance and pleasure of struggle and competition and testing; it insists that the individual is never merely a pawn of his world but always one of its coproducers. Despite its stress upon agency, however, its commitment to fairness means a consistent judgment upon the manipulative and exploitative character of action in the everyday world.

Playing argues that, at least for the moment, the "real" is illusory and the "illusory" is real, and it judges the structures of this world tentative and provisional in the same movement by which it grasps new possibilities that can heal the self or temporarily redeem the times. But it is always a dialectical affirmation and rejection of the world as we know it, denying the actual only in the name of possibilities that the actual enshrines. It rejects finite imperfections and pretensions to ultimacy, but it still affirms structure and therefore provides no license for feelings of anomie. It acknowledges the irrepressible appetite of the self for more than the factual order, for more than society can offer, but it does this in a fashion that deepens the bonds of community instead of threatening them. At least from the corner of its eye, it regards even the stranger as a potential participant in the game and never as simply or forever a spectator. We can play alone, of course, and often we do; few defenses against the lures and cruelties of the world are as important and beneficial as solitary but not lonely play. On the other hand, playing together has traditionally served as a primary instrument of socialization in the West. It brings people to a common place, enforces upon them common rules and goals, teaches them to respect limits and fairness and the many exigencies of life together, and implants a sense of community that recognizes as brothers in the same game even those who play on different teams.

Among the most important aspects of the image are its implications for our perception of time and space. It is not so much the fault of our readiness to measure ourselves in terms of the objects for which we have bartered ourselves as it is our bondage to time quantified, to minutes and hours and days measured mechanically by the ticking of the clock, that has chained us so tightly to a less than human realm. In playing, however, the reign of time quantified is always provisional and subject to interruption, while in some varieties of play a whole new mode of temporality emerges. Then time is measured in accordance with the rhythms of the human heart, and in this triumph of small *kairoi* over the tyranny of *kronos* there is a reflection and anticipation of the *kairos* of the presence of God. Then, too, especially within the arts, play can lay hold of epiphanies of the future without regard for ordinary canons of probability, and these intimations can have their impact upon conscience in the present, endowing our actual possibilities with new amplitude. Much the same is true for our understanding of space; playing establishes some relatively inviolable and private sphere where man is exempt from the ordinary publicizing of life that suggests he is no more than a function of society and of its routines. On the other hand, it can also remedy our isolation in space, either bringing the present generation together or else enabling the self to populate the place where it dwells by means of imaginative identification with other generations long since dead or yet unborn.

Furthermore, play manages to reconcile in some organic fashion the divergent impulses of Dionysus and Apollo, dynamics and form, by displaying the many ways that the affirmation of order is intrinsic to the expression of vitality. Structure is embraced for the sake of the actualization of all the wildness and wilderness of human passion, and in this affirmation order is accepted in an act of choice and freedom, not encountered simply as fate. Players learn to recognize in a code or discipline not an arbitrary and external authority but the indispensable resources for the maintenance of the game. In the same way, playing demonstrates the integral connection of *animus* and *anima*, fulfillment and sacrifice, victory and submission, the affirmation and the denial of the self. When we play together, there can be no satisfaction of one impulse unless the other also finds what it desires. Playing includes and affirms what the self is and what it is intended to become, the natural impulse to play that is shared with other animals and the distinctively human principle of fairness. It includes the aged as well as the young, for the precincts of memory provide fertile fields for play to recapture; no one is excluded by the impairment of faculties or loss of functions.

Play can train us to compensate for the poverty of imagination that afflicts our society and that is the root of our greatest failures in individual and corporate moral life. Sometimes a brief and commonplace affair, sometimes the genesis of our greatest art and innovation, playing remains the best testimony that man is a creature made for more than the world can provide. The image meets a variety of needs and addresses a wide range of phenomena in what it has to tell about the companionship of youth and age, the involution of vitality and form, the inseparability of liberty and law, our opportunities to redeem the structures of time and space, the congruence of natural impulse and historical destiny, the achievement of privacy together with the inclusion of all within the same game, the limits of the factual order and the appetite for more than it can offer. Then, too, the interpretation of the self as player lessens the threats to personal identity that are posed by times of crisis or massive social change. The image cautions us against any undialectical identification with either the old or the new in the social world.

How persuasive is the "empirical fit" of the image will always remain a question for debate. But at least it can serve, when complemented by other imagery, as a fair expression of the anthropological implications of the Christian story, and it can be read in ways that are faithful to the principle of fairness that rational selves must affirm. So faith kindled by the presence of God bears with it a master image that justifies the dictates of temperance, courage, and justice and that liberates the self to act on the principle of fairness, because the image implies the reality of a sphere of basic trust. From a Christian point of view, all the virtues are bound up with one another and with the reality of revelation, just as the human stands always in relation to the holy. God dwells in eternity, however, while man lives in time and time lives in man. So there are times for the player to play one game and times for him to play another, some moments for struggle and others for rest, some occasions to accept responsibility and other times when responsibility is best yielded to God. As the Preacher wrote:

> For everything there is a season, and a time for every matter under heaven:
> A time to be born, and a time to die;
> A time to plant, and a time to pluck up what is planted;
> A time to kill, and a time to heal;
> A time to break down, and a time to build up;
> A time to weep, and a time to laugh;
> A time to mourn, and a time to dance;
> A time to cast away stones, and a time to gather stones together;
> A time to embrace, and a time to refrain from embracing;
> A time to seek, and a time to lose;
> A time to keep, and a time to cast away;
> A time to rend, and a time to sew;
> A time to keep silence, and a time to speak;
> A time to love, and a time to hate;
> A time for war, and a time for peace.
>
> —Ecclesiastes 3:1-8

If we are to discern the times, spy out all the rhythms of the actual, listen to all the different music that the world plays, then a final virtue is necessary: prudence. On its presence depends the welfare of the other virtues. Prudence offers life or else withholds it from them all. The principle of fairness, the image of the player, the story that enriches the image and enforces the principle: none will serve us if our prudence does not serve them.

9

prudence and god

On first acquaintance, prudence appears to be unlike the other virtues and less significant; indeed, it seems to describe virtuosity rather than virtue, a skill similar to whistling or to the expertise of a carpenter. It is important, however, because we have no way to know what justice and courage will actually demand of us apart from the particular situations that call for their practice. The virtues will scarcely be virtuous if they are not related to the changing contexts of the self. Just as someone can know a great deal about justice and still not practice it, so also in the name of justice can a person barge hurriedly into a situation in some abrupt fashion that will violate the privacy and rights of everyone involved. Prudence expresses the situational aspect of moral life, sensitivity toward the density and specificity and all the unrepeatable particularity of whatever is here and now, and this is knowledge that we must acquire if we are really to serve principles that transcend any single time or place. Prudence is so bound to the finite and definite that it will not dare to ask about all that is possible, but so bound, too, that it will know what is appropriate. What is fitting, here and now? How can it be achieved? What are the exigencies of justice or courage or temperance at this particular place at four o'clock in the afternoon? Prudence denotes the skills, in thought and practice alike, without which principles will never be translated satisfactorily from the pages of books into the daily commerce of man with man. Its meaning, therefore, is *a sense of the situation.*

But little is understood of prudence if it is identified simply with skill at devising means, implementing ends, defining situations, and judging the form in which the virtues can be realized in different contexts. It refers to the whole relationship of the self with actuality, with whatever is possibly real or really possible. We will never understand a particular situation unless it is relativized and illuminated by its context in the history of our commerce with reality. Prudence is the turning point of the world of the individual, the place of a *coincidentia oppositorum* where many things that first seem opposed display their integral connections and affinities—contemplation and action, the internal and the external, moral selfhood and the artist's venture, selfless regard and love, losing life and finding it again, the human and the holy. To speak of prudence is to affirm that the first moral task is not to remake the world but simply to see how the world is made, to find a way to travel so far from the snarls and tangles of absorption with the self that we can see and join the world as it really is. There will be little chance to remake anything at all until we have learned to see it for what it is.

Virtue means the sort of integrity and consistency and wholeness that the self must achieve for itself, although the achievement is impossible without the gifts that others provide. Human excellence will be less than human if it fails to include an aesthetic as well as a moral component, and nowhere else is this as apparent as it is in prudence. The virtue denotes the congruence of the eye with actuality. It demands something akin to *aisthēsis*, a way of seeing that cares above all else for the particularity and individuality of the persons and things and situations that the self confronts. Whenever the aesthetic and moral aspects of life are treated as though they were two different realms, we lose touch with the unity of the self and the relatedness of its experience. There is a paradigm of what prudence involves in what is sometimes called aesthetic apprehension, the sort of perceiving that is elicited from us or enforced upon us by the presence of a work of art that has been crafted to trap our attention upon its own immanent meanings and values, in all of their immediacy and without reference to anything beyond themselves. There are differences, of course, because aesthetic apprehension has no end beyond itself and the pleasure it affords, while the vision that prudence requires is meant to serve the interests of fairness, to assure responsive congruence and conformity with what the actual is seen to be and to deserve. But they share a disinterestedness, a concern for the object simply because it is *there*, a willingness to see it disclose what it is in its own time and in its own way.

It is the misfortune of the self, however, that the persons and things it confronts were not fashioned as works of art to trap and rapture our senses. Other selves function in many ways for us, but they do not ordinarily function as aesthetic objects. New situations place many demands upon us, but they rarely honor our request that they remain unchanged and unchanging until we can scrutinize them at leisure. Western philosophy has sometimes spoken of beauty as a transcendental attribute of all that is actual, but our vision does not often strike so deeply into things that it is held within the vise of the beauty there. Most of our commerce with reality is cursory and partial, dictated by no more than what pleasure or utility demands, and so furnishing us with nothing except whatever is required by the apparent necessities of the everyday world or approved by its social constraints. We fall into the confusion of similarity with sameness, accepting the validity of old stereotypes and assumptions in new situations, hastening always onward, or at least somewhere, yet never encountering anything new or even the depths of the old because we have not prepared ourselves to see what is really there. Our habitual indifference and the particular enervation of age, the small aches and sudden pains that clot attention upon the self, the weight of convention and bite of xenophobia, all of our dismal and fantastic preoccupations, the demands for decision that afford no leisure to sift and weigh what should be known before decisions are reached —all of these and much else distract us from the mystery of the particularity of things and from the particularity of the mystery of man.

Thomas Aquinas writes of the way that the Christian virtue of charity becomes the form of all the virtues by means of its impact upon prudence. His comments are faithful to the most fundamental dimension of moral life, for there can be no prudence at all without love, love in the sense of imaginative sensitivity toward what lies beyond the self. Again we encounter the circularity that consistently appears in the exploration of virtue: There can be no prudence without love; there can be no love or justice or any other virtue appropriately expressed without prudence. Even when it is regarded as no more than a skill, prudence still depends upon a basic disposition of the self, upon a vitality of imagination that only love can fire. Consequently, the analogy between the prudent self and someone who is ingested by the world of a work of art fails, because one depends much more than the other upon the fundamental orientation, character, or disposition of the individual. A better analogy exists between the artist himself and what prudence demands. As R. G. Collingwood wrote many years ago, "One paints a thing in order to see it. . . . A good painter—any good painter will tell you the same—paints things because until he has painted them he doesn't know what they are like."[1] Perhaps Collingwood was too sanguine about the unanimity of the opinions of painters, but it is true nonetheless that the perceptions embodied in the arts turn our vision outward, initiate us to some of the exigencies of prudence, and judge the magnitude of its absence from our everyday lives. Collingwood calls us to recognize that it is never easy to see, that vision requires time and energy, humility and patience and creativeness. Where love is lacking, what reason remains for tasks so difficult?

Nowhere else is the unity of virtue so apparent as it is in the workings of prudence. Just as it includes love in the form of imaginative sensitivity or empathy, so does it presuppose some versions of faith. There can be no just and objective regard for actuality if the relationships of the self have not endowed it with the faith that discerns a realm of basic trust within which it is liberated from obsession with its own contingency and from the lust for security. Because reality includes the possible as well as the actual, prudence kindles hope and hope encourages prudence. But the faith and hope and love that undergird prudence all gain their vitality and health from what others have given to us, and so it is that our vision of actuality is shaped for better and for worse by the treatment we receive within the human enterprise. On the other hand, prudence is the only tutor we have to tell us what we can hope for, when faith is misplaced, how love can be appropriately and justly expressed.

The counsel to play fair will finally drift as far from our condition as a star on a cold winter night unless it is drawn back to the earth by the magnet of a prudent perception of others who are involved in our game. Without prudence, its companion virtues wander off the world and into realms of fantasy—and yet, how could the self ever see justly if it were not already trained and habituated in what justice means? Stanley Hauerwas is entirely persuasive when he argues:

The problem with situation ethics is that in spite of its claim to provide men with autonomy it is working with a very passive model of the self. The self is always lost amid the contingencies of the particular situation. For men to have autonomy in any meaningful sense they must be able to meet "the situation" on grounds other than that provided by it. Such grounds must be based on their character.[2]

We have no way to assess whether or not we see justly unless we have antecedently learned what temperance and justice and courage involve. We are not autonomous if our acts are dictated by others or by the hegemony of abstractions, of course; they must be indisputably our own and shaped to fit the contours of particular situations. But neither will we be autonomous unless we bring to the situation some knowledge of what fair play means and do not rely entirely on the uninformed instruction of the context. If we are moral selves, this knowledge will be embodied in some sort of fundamental direction or intentionality or character. Prudence cannot stand alone, then, and neither can anything else. Every dissection of the virtues, unfortunately, every attempt to place them in order and rank, does violence to the unity and dynamism of their life.

The greatest distraction from what prudence requires is simply ourselves, the problem of our inherent selfishness, our unwillingness to look at what we do not want to see and the intervention of the self between its own gaze and what it does want to see. In its consequences for moral life, our plight reflects not the limits of knowledge but the reality of sin, not the creative role of mind in transforming and ordering the opaque stuff of experience but the occlusion of the eye of the mind because the self is forever standing in its own way. The eye becomes a mirror instead of a window, and reality is covered over by a thousand fractured images of the self. So existence dwindles to a diminishing routine of self-assertions because now there is nothing to see except the self, and to a succession of strategies to find security, for in this realm of illusion there is comfortable lodging for the final illusion of security.

Aquinas writes of covetousness as the principal enemy of prudence, and in his work it becomes a metaphor that includes every attempt of the self to be its own god. The spoilage of vision that it involves is reflected in the ambition to purchase our own security and in the capacity for deceit, especially for the deception of the self, without which the ambition would find no room to root. Covetousness leads to the betrayal of trust because it is grounded in the absence of basic trust. Precisely because it will not or cannot envision a realm of basic trust, it finds its primary antagonists in process and in becoming, for it knows no reason why change should be interpreted to mean more than accident and contingency and randomness. So it lusts after a false aseity, a stationary world in the sense that while more quantity can be admitted there is no room for qualitative change. Prudence, on the other hand, means the end of all covetousness, for only when the self is willing to lose itself can it find its world, and only there—hard up against the dynamism and the actuality of which it is a part—can it ever gain itself. Josef Pieper comments:

> Covetousness means an anxious senility, desperate self-preservation, over-riding concern for confirmation and security. Need we say how utterly contrary such an attitude is to the fundamental bent of prudence; how impossible the informed and receptive silence of the subject before the truth of real things, how impossible just estimate and decision is, without a youthful spirit of brave trust and, as it were, a reckless tossing away of anxious self-preservation, a relinquishment of all egoistic bias toward mere confirmation of the self; how utterly, therefore, the virtue of prudence is dependent upon the constant readiness to ignore the self, the limberness of real humility and objectivity.[3]

There is a profound and important connection between coveting and boredom. Prudence carries us into the midst of the world and involves us in its processes of becoming. Covetousness is suspicious of becoming, and so it paves the way for boredom that reflects the ways in which we have exiled ourselves from participation in the dynamics of life. Boredom means that becoming has stopped for this particular self, at least for an hour or perhaps for a day or perhaps until the day of death. At the root of the problem there is an absence of basic trust, gutting our willingness to risk and dare and test ourselves because we can see in the processes of becoming no sense, no coherence, nothing but futility and randomness. Sometimes the self is intent upon certain possibilities that cannot be realized in a particular situation, and so it willfully averts its eyes from the potentiality that is really there: I will not see and I am bored. Sometimes we fail to grasp the possibilities of the moment because the self is standing in front of itself, and so everything grows as stale and flat as this individual who is his own barrier against actuality: I cannot see and I am bored. Sometimes our habit of measuring the self in terms of the things it owns, the image it projects, and the respect it commands can blind us to the possibilities within the individual that are most richly and distinctively human, and so we cease to become as selves: there is no I to see and, now with greater reason, boredom shadows and distances the realm of the actual.

Sometimes it is simply the busyness of life that first evokes and then as quickly manages to mask the boredom caused by our passive suffering of the ways that the everyday world plunders the potentialities most singularly and specially our own. Sometimes it arises from our selfishness or enervation, sometimes its source lies in what seems superficially the too familiar or too enigmatic visage that reality presents to us, but always boredom fails to pierce the mystery of becoming that surrounds us and so, alongside despair, it stands at the farthest distance possible from the sense of the presence of that which alone is supremely actual. It is difficult to remedy, for it saps the strength that the quest for a remedy in prudence requires. Still, there are times when we are confronted and confounded by the presence of otherness and then engrafted despite ourselves into the richer imagination or wilder hoping of a child or friend, unselfed by another self and so rescued from our momentary death of self.

Boredom will visit us again, though, for it is the penalty that coveting reaps, thereby receiving more than even it coveted, and covetousness is the fundamental expression of our universal estrangement from the holy. If it is evident in our passion for things, it is no less apparent in our ecstatic and sometimes sacrificial identification with greater powers and causes, for in all these we seek to find ourselves. Covetousness testifies that the ambition of the self to find its own life will end with the loss of life, for in one way or another the search deprives men of access to the dynamics of the world. Man is Antaeus, everywhere and always; the classical image of the unity of man and world gains resonance from the Christian conviction that the holy is found nowhere except amidst the ambiguities of the earth. In the boredom and dessicated imagination that inform so much of contemporary life, and in their reflections in our indiscriminate chasing of excitement that acknowledges no difference between breaking a window or carrying off the rails from a country bridge or firing a shotgun from a speeding car at the back of some unknown child, there is a fine gauge of how very far our culture has distanced itself from the holy.

In the Western tradition, the good has been identified with the actual, evil with the deprivation of actuality where it ought to be, the source of goodness with the supremely actual, and God himself has been understood to be involved in the processes of becoming. Prudence is first among the virtues because it means conformity and congruence with the actual; it provides access to the concrete and specific details of the movement of life. Man is made for union and communion with other selves and with the world itself; he cannot violate his destiny except at the price of the loss of the self. If prudence does not lead him toward it, then boredom is inevitable because now the self is alone with itself and isolated from what its nature most desires. Sometimes there are metaphysical grounds for boredom, of course, as in the instance of a small child who simply does not yet possess the resources to entertain himself for long when he is left alone. Nevertheless, in any phenomenology of estrangement written from the perspective of the idea of virtue, boredom demands special attention. Sartre has told us that hell is other people, but this is true precisely because we no longer see anything except images of ourselves reflected in their eyes, endlessly reflected and endlessly boring and endlessly barring us from access again to the mystery of becoming.

In a sense, prudence is the most theological of all the virtues, ushering us from our seats among the audience to the stage where the drama of the human and the holy is played. The realm of the finite and definite has its own intrinsic significance and independent worth, and the often unrepeatable particularity within it seems all the more beautiful because everything is so ephemeral and, once lost, can never be retrieved. But all things also stand in relationship to a power that transcends the world. The holy dwells at the roots of the self as well as beyond its highest aspirations, and, insofar as vision really conforms with actuality, the self travels nearer to the presence of God. Pieper writes that the eyes of faith are aware

of deeper dimensions of reality, to which the eyes of the average man and the average Christian are not yet opened. To those who have this greater love of God the truth of real things is revealed more plainly and more brilliantly; above all the supernatural reality of the Trinitarian God is made known to them more movingly and overwhelmingly. Even supreme supernatural prudence, however, can have only the following aim: to make the more deeply felt truth of the reality of God and world the measure for will and action. Man can have no other standard and signpost than things as they are and the truth which makes manifest things as they are; and there can be no higher standard than the God who is and his truth.[4]

In each new contact with actuality, the self adds to the skein of its relationships with that which is supremely actual, even though man may know nothing of what he does. In each new contact, too, there are opportunities to actualize possibilities that even God himself could not realize in the same fashion as the terminal finite individual. From a Christian perspective, however, the obverse of the theological dimension of prudence is the difficulty of its attainment. The eye falters, gaze is averted, the ineradicable selfishness of the self blurs vision of him in whom the self finds fulfillment only by surrender.

In the end, prudence depends not only upon what we can do for ourselves but equally upon what the world does with us. In some measure, of course, our vision can be refashioned by our own efforts, and the habit of attention to reality can triumph over some of the constraints and blindnesses born of our selfishness or the conventions of the everyday. But then there are times when our symbolic universe is shaken and weighed, invaded and found wanting, turned all upside down because there is nowhere to run from actuality and it is too much for us. The tides of reality lash against our defenses, and we have no strength left to fight their erosion; all the carefully tilled fields of imagination are flooded, and within the house that mind has built it seems as though not one stone is left upon another. These are the crisis times—it may be a birth or a birthday, an unexpected parting or a move to a new town or a visit to a foreign land—when suddenly the world as we have seen it is supplanted by a new one, sometimes simpler but more exigent, sometimes more complex and labyrinthine, always more alien and contingent than we would have dreamed.

There are also all the occasions when another self meets us as "thou," marvelously occupying the whole range of our vision, calling us to acknowledge the brute and obdurate otherness that informs reality and inviting us once again to the remarkable discovery that someone else is just as real as oneself. Sometimes, too, perception is healed and unselfed within the Christian community, if it manages to serve not only as mediator but also as the sort of forum in which one must accept and affirm the presence of the other and the indescribable otherness of presence. In ways many and various, sometimes small and beautiful and sometimes irremediably tragic, reality forces us to face the truth that we are not alone. There is the other and the other world that he sees and within which he is destined to make his choices—that alien territory encroaching upon our own, judging and relativizing our universe, tilting it a bit so that it no longer seems familiar and thereby luring us out again to engage in the constant struggle of learning to see.

In this power of the world to draw us beyond ourselves there is an intimation of grace; we meet a presence or an event and it is able to unchain us from ourselves, forcing us away from our own preoccupations not in order to serve alien ends but simply in order that we can reach out and touch what is actually there, surrounding us but never noticed before. This is the deepest root of humility: it is founded not so much upon a modest regard for our own talents or on a recognition of the magnitude of the sacrifices of others, but just on the dazzling revelation that there are all sorts of realities in the world, all sorts of centers from which it is organized, and the I is no more than one among an endless array. Sometimes the world exerts its power from the lodging it has found in memory, as remembering calls us away from a land darkened by the shadow of the self and restores the objective regard that, perhaps a bit romantically, we associate with childhood. So it is both an act of prudence and preparation to pursue the virtue if we can guard the rectitude of remembering; it, too, is as much subject to spoilage as everything else domiciled within the self, and it lends its resources quickly to our ventures in the deception of ourselves. Pieper quite properly warns:

> The virtue of prudence resides in this: that the objective cognition of reality shall determine action; that the truth of real things shall become determinative. This truth of real things, however, is contained in the true-to-being memory. . . . There is no

more insidious way for error to establish itself than by this falsi-
fication of the memory through slight retouches, displacements,
discolorations, omissions, shifts of accent.[5]

As memory touches the shores of childhood again, the epiphanies of grace that it rediscovers disclose and reaffirm their significance for the development of the unselfed regard on which every
virtue hangs: when young eyes are caught by a worm unravelling
itself across a leaf, or by the splinters of dazzle on the surface of a
stream, by the paint caught in someone else's hair or the globed
brilliance of a wet spider web struck by the sun. The intentness of
a little girl alone with her imagination and raptured by a game
that no one else can see or a boy caught up in the geometry of a
bird across the sky—such simple things add together and can
provide the sort of *praeparatio evangelii* from which prudence
comes. The rectitude of memory is priceless; without it we lose
touch with ourselves and with the narrative of our lives. Then,
too, the shared memories of our different communities afford the
only lodging there is for the great stories that inform and grant
significance to the small narrative of the individual. If memory
plays false with us, the stories are twisted and diminished, and by
that much are our possibilities of action curtailed.

But no matter how often or savagely the world shakes us out
of our absorption with ourselves, its powers of disclosure still
depend upon a cleansing of the household of the mind that no one
else and no power of the world can accomplish for us. What we
can see is shaped by the store of images we hold, and so the
perennial problem of prudence is to sweep up and sort out the
stable of the imagination. An immaculate imagination is even more
unlikely than an immaculate conception, however; prudence
remains haunted and crippled by phantoms and daimons born
from our visions of strength that do not recognize our frailty or
our images of impotence that do not acknowledge our responsibility. Precisely because it is potentially the most theological of all
the virtues, because it demands more resolute selflessness than any
of the rest, no other virtue is so elusive and difficult to achieve.

As Boulding recognizes, prudent impressions of the world are
not awarded free access to consciousness; they are modified and
tailored, minimized or stressed, quickly embraced or stubbornly
resisted by scales of valuation already resident in the constellation

of images that comprise our symbolic universe. That universe is as far fallen as the individual and social histories which it illuminates but from which it has also been derived. Stories can be supplanted by other stories, images can be displaced by new images, but still a residue of the old will remain in the ways that consciousness is scored and channel marked; habitual patterns of valuation retain a sort of ghostly presence amidst the new. So the problem is not simply that of the substitution of the full Christian story for bits and shards of other tales.

One of the requisites of prudence is a symbolic universe sufficiently plastic and unfinished that it can yield to new perceptions that conflict with some of the old, a universe that awards high value to novelty, challenge, and change but that can still subject them to critical scrutiny. We need a symbolic universe that prepares the self to undertake any game, no matter how unlikely, but we also need to acknowledge that there are rules which pertain to every game and cannot be abrogated for the sake of any particular form of play. We need an image of the self that displays the self-transcendent character of our humanness, too, recalling us to our endless capacity to choose to be more than and other than we are today, or are ever in the realm of the everyday. Still another requisite of this image is that it must qualify the seriousness of all our "serious" pursuits, dispute the seriousness of the claims levied upon us without denying either the extent or the importance of our obligations. It must display the relativity of our values and the limitations of our perspectives so that we can loosen our grip on all of these but still not let them go; in other words, it must enable us to retrieve the dialectic in our faiths and hopes and loves. The image of the player provides one way, at least, to satisfy these needs. Not only can it convey the anthropological implications of the disclosure of God, not only can it express what temperance and justice and courage involve, but it can also transform the symbolic universe of the self so that consciousness proves hospitable to the discoveries of unselfed and prudent regard.

Prudence cares for words, for their weight and specificity and nuances and ambiguities, because words are the stuff from which images are formed. Language brings order and clarity to experience, and it is so much involved in the cognitive process that words themselves are always part of the material with which intellect works, inseparable from the flow of impressions that they decipher for the self. Because linguistic usage is an act of world creation that either expands or constricts the realm within which we are free to choose, prudence must busy itself with the exigencies of speaking truly and well. It must flee from the generalities and abstractions and conventions that reaffirm the tyranny of the everyday world and enforce ways of seeing that rob men of opportunities for fresh and sustained contact with reality.

Among the preparations necessary if we are to speak well there is the need for silence, for listening, for offering to actuality the respect that allows it to disclose itself for what it is in its own time and manner. Listening and keeping silence can be a small thing, but it is among the greatest of human acts in its expression of man's true situation in the world, as no more than one creature among many, all of whom stand in the presence of God. Whenever we confuse laziness with simply doing nothing for a while, or silence with having nothing at all to say, we diminish our chances to grasp reality and by that much we diminish ourselves. The world has its own rhythms of disclosure; sometimes we cannot hasten them, and we shall not hear them if we do not practice listening and learn to keep still. We are deaf to intimations at the best of times, and in large measure because our approach to reality is so thoroughly manipulative; the occasional habit of silence is a significant remedy for that, and for our selfishness as well. There is a real dialectic again in the relationship of speech and silence: if we do not keep silence, we will have nothing important to say; if our speech is too coarse or shallow to sculpture a world of clarity and different dimensions, there is little reason to keep silence before it and listen. One of the most curious of the bourgeois aberrations that have afflicted the idea of virtue is the notion that the prudent man is timid, unwilling to give offense, committed to uncontroversial speech. On the contrary, when he is slow to speak it is only because he cares to speak truly; his allegiance is not to any sort of community, or to community at any price, but to the truth of the way things really are.

When prudence is baptized by Christian faith, its primary meaning is a sense of timeliness, skill at deciphering when the time is right. It is true that prudence describes all of the faithful contact of the self with actuality, but actuality is process, becoming, transition, and change. The self must know when and where and how to respond to the presence and activity of the supremely actual, for at least within the Christian tradition it is not believed that God is equally near to all places or equally present at all times. When there is no sense of the right time, so that the appointments of the creature with his lord go unrecognized or are wrongly understood, there is nothing to invest the imagery of faith with new luminosity and persistence. The keeping of faith shrinks to faith in faith, love falls to praise of love, and hoping for things not seen sinks to hoping in hope itself, good old American optimism. Beginning as a skill required for the autonomy of man, prudence ends as the key to participation in a divine work. On the one hand, it signifies the ability to resolve a moral problem and answer the question of the form of virtuous action in a particular context. On the other, it describes the way to partnership in a theological mystery, when intimations of the holy provoke men to act in ways that reason might condone but certainly would never counsel by itself.

These two meanings of the virtue, apparently so disparate, are inseparably related, at least for Christian eyes. The self is called to moral agency in a world where God is active, but the intent of that activity is to afford and maintain for man a realm for the free expanse of his own potentialities and creativeness, a sphere where man must decide for himself what prudence demands. There the self is called to play fair. But playing fair is no sufficient compensation for what we have been given by parents or children or friends; nor is it all that is needed by the haunted and wretched of the earth. Fair play is not much of a response to the plight of a retarded child. When prudence has been instructed by Christian faith in the characteristic mode of divine activity, the sacrificial and creative love manifest in the cross and resurrection of Jesus Christ, it offers justice what justice sought but could not offer to itself— the greater wisdom called *agape*. The supremely actual to which all else is related is love; in, with, and under the actualities of the earth he lures us beyond what the virtues strictly counsel and enchants the heart in a responsive love for whatever it is that he has made.

Timeliness means the recovery of our ability to recognize that there are *kairoi* for rest and for labor, for dancing and for contemplation, for shouting and keeping still, for protest and submission—as well as certain times made right by the presence of God. It frees us from servitude to the mechanized world we built to serve ourselves, from the measurement of what has breath and spontaneity in terms so alien that maturity becomes an affair of the calendar instead of the man. Time is no more beaten flat, deprived of its real topography, squeezed dry of its essential elements of music and rhythm until it is not fit for human habitation. Impatience and lethargy seem strange companions, but in a quantified world they march to the same tune and force us to join their march. Impatience wants everything now, all in a heap; it wants to savor anticipation and realization in the same moment. Affluence makes much that once seemed an extraordinary treat now a commonplace, and so the self is deprived of the elements of tension, expectation, and struggle that provide some of its essential nourishment. Now nothing seems to come at the right time or at the end of an hour's game. The consequence, of course, is boredom, lethargy, and then apathy, until tedium becomes too great to be borne and impatience begins to gnaw at the bones of the self again. Life disintegrates into a chaos of violent wishes and sudden gestures, then equally sudden enervation and the death of wishing; and then again the search begins for excitement instead of challenge, for something new instead of something good.

What is masked by the quest for novelty is a more elemental passion, however, the thirst for a mode of time that coincides with the rhythms of the heart, that is more human and humanizing than what is offered by the clock, and that can renew man's contact with the movements of his world. Where *kronos* rules, this policeman of the everyday, the diminution of man means the diminution of nature, too. Time quantified divorces man from his environment and destroys his old sense of kinship, thereby offering its own contribution to the exploitation of the earth. But the sense of timeliness acknowledges that man is brother to the world in which he lives, that he too has a time to be born and to die, to plant and to harvest, to test his strength and to confess his frailty, to rise up and to lie down. The most creative of human acts, reconciliation with others and with the earth, the binding together of what has been broken, requires a knowledge of the right time no less than it demands love. One must know when approach will threaten and be called trespass, when concern will seem no more than prying, and when a gesture of affection or penitence will strike to another's heart and bring him to community again.

There is no reason to wait, no reason to counsel patience, if time cannot be measured except by the clock, for then there will never be a right time. William Lynch properly comments that "the decision to wait is one of the great human acts," for by its own choice the self "gives the future the only chance it has to emerge. It is, therefore, the most fundamental act, not the least act, of the imagination."[6] On the one hand, it is an act of faith in the future and in the powers that will shape the future, including the agency of one's own self: it is the strongest affirmation of tomorrow, indeed, that a man can make. On the other, it need not be an uncritical affirmation; we shall wait and see. Novelty itself is not a value, so we shall wait to weigh and assess the situation that emerges next week and, by that scrutiny, insist upon the autonomy of the self. Waiting is an acknowledgment that man is unfinished, unfinished in the sense that the imagination opens itself to receive additional resources and assistance from others, refusing to become inflexible or constricted and a prisoner of its own past.

Not least important, the decision to wait is worlds removed from the desperate constraint that sometimes seizes us to realize every possibility the day affords because time marches on; Monday we must return to the office again, and next autumn we shall be forty years old. Less often realized than not, there is a tacit assumption in this frenzy of activity and incessant search for pleasure that the world is godless, and therefore no power except the power of man is available to realize the ephemeral possibilities that existence holds. Sometimes, a sense of the situation simply counsels men to wait until a better time for action comes. Sometimes, however, the sense of timeliness grows to become an act of faith in the presence and activity of the holy, a looking forward not to a right time in the affairs of men but to a time made right by the affairs of God. Then the decision to wait is a Passover meal eaten with staff in hand, a preparation so that the crucial appointment will not be missed. Anticipation offers rebirth to necessary images and mends the nets of sensibility until waiting becomes a creative act.

The right time is disclosed not only in what the eye perceives, though, but also in what resounds within the chambers of the ear —an unfamiliar intonation, a hurried footstep, a voice that arises from some unknown corner within the self, the pleas for attention disguised beneath the conventionalities of ordinary discourse. Somehow the occasional music and ordinary cacophony of human encounter are not captured as readily or as immediately by our imaging and imagining as they are in the times when we do nothing but listen or when the voice of another self suddenly shreds our defenses against interruption. There is a biblical story about an encounter of Moses with the holy that serves as a paradigm of all the commerce between man and God.

> Moses said, "I pray thee, show me thy glory." And he said, "I will make all my goodness pass before you, and will proclaim before you my name 'The Lord'; and I will be gracious to whom I will be gracious, and will show mercy on whom I will show mercy. But," he said, "you cannot see my face; for man shall not see me and live." And the Lord said, "Behold, there is a place by me where you shall stand upon the rock; and while my glory passes by I will put you in a cleft of the rock, and I will cover you with my hand until I have passed by; then I will take away my hand, and you shall see my back; but my face shall not be seen."
>
> —Exodus 33:18-23

The Lord engages his creatures in speech, tells them his name, and summons some of them to speak to their brothers on his behalf. His transactions with men invest our common speech with a new freight of significance. Our experience of the words of others awakens us to the mystery of elements of the self that do not dwell within its words, and this small instance of transcendence can provide a bit of confirmation of the truthfulness of others when they are commissioned to speak to us of God. But man can never see God; every disclosure of the holy is an exercise in iconoclasm, when images are exposed as potential idols and broken because there is no truth, or at least no undialectical truth, in the analogies they are intended to convey.

When we enter a new situation, spend a vacation somewhere we have never been before or visit a foreign land, the self suffers from a process of selective vision: the eye will absorb no more than whatever the mind and heart can accept. Selective vision is one of the sources of the strangeness of memory; someone who shared our experiences remembers them differently, omitting much that we noticed, stressing something that entirely passed us by. It is a necessary measure of protection in a poor and alien land: deformities that in familiar surroundings would have arrested us in pity and shock are not seen, deprivation that would have seemed a scandal now provokes no comment, a child whose hands were sliced away by his mother so that he could beg for a living seems to represent nothing except another of nature's ways. Sometimes one of these wretched ones is not content to keep her distance, though, and rubs a scabrous, brittle arm, so surprisingly thin, against our own. That alien touch recalls us from ourselves so that we must listen to the rising tenor of her whine, her voice more shrill than unctuous now, and heed her practiced desperation. Her touch opens our ears, and what the eye could ignore a moment ago the ear can no longer evade. Sight had left us outside the situation, invulnerable and unmoved; after all, the eye must distance something from itself in order to bring it into focus. But now touch and hearing conspire together and bring us nearer than vision can, drawing us inside the circle of her need.

As Christians understand their condition, the selective vision of the traveler haunts him just as much when he walks along familiar streets, and one of its names is sin. When the holy raptures a person beyond himself and into a strange and foreign land, the self still carries with it the baggage of all that it has been, going into the new world laden with all the old ways of perceiving. Because we can exercise choice and agency only within the world that we can see, however, even in the new country our lives are not very different from what they have always been. The land is not terra incognita, really, for the familiar old shadow of the self lies across everything we see. In a different sense, of course, this is an unknown land, for the self is standing in the way of its own vision still. However great the habit of virtue, there remains an inexpugnable selfishness that spoils our sight and, as Augustine knew, threatens the transformation of the virtues into splendid vices and nothing more.

Vision always depends upon images; we cannot elude our condition and function without them. Even when the world somehow manages to unself our sight, that does not conquer the selectivity of imagination or abbreviate the distance that focus requires or hold selfishness long at bay. What we need is not the displacement of the eye by the ear, for blindness is no virtue, but a new store of imagery that can augment the old, images of hearing that can instruct us by pointing to where there is a voice worth hearing always, by telling how it can best be heard, by showing what faithful listening involves. The remedy for the problems of distance and selectivity will not be found entirely within the realm of images, of course, but only in the midst of all the realities they are meant to clarify and interpret. Nevertheless, images of faithful listening can prepare us better to hear the words of others and a word from beyond them, and so draw us closer together until we can begin to touch one another again. Virtue is the best that man can do for himself, and even for that he must rely consistently upon others. But virtue itself counsels that beyond virtue lies something greater, and for that man can rely only upon God. Vision itself calls for the complement of the other senses, and so there is a time for transition from these fragmentary explorations of images that clarify sight to the story of other images that can sharpen hearing and soften touch. Then the dictates of fair play are affirmed and surpassed if we learn, before God, what it means to play by ear.

notes

Introduction

1. This essay will certainly be misunderstood if it is not remembered that while I write as a Christian, the scope of the inquiry includes far less than the substance of Christian teaching about the matters at hand. For example, in the discussion of the structure of faith and love, there is no systematic consideration of faith as knowledge of God or of love as *amor crucis*. The essay remains within the province of a *Christian natural theology*, as that phrase is here defined.
2. "Plausibility structure" is a phrase borrowed from Peter L. Berger, although I do not believe there has been any single structure that has long included a great majority of the populace of the West. In chapter 6 I want to avoid an intellectualistic distortion of the notion, and therefore I interpret it as a continuing complex of shared *experiences* given similar readings by different people because of a common system of symbols. Cf. Berger, *The Sacred Canopy* (New York: Doubleday, 1967), especially chapters 2 and 6.
3. Dietrich von Oppen, *The Age of the Person* (Philadelphia: Fortress Press, 1969), pp. 38-39. Used by permission.

Chapter 1. Habits

1. Albert Camus, *The Plague* (New York: Knopf, 1964), tr. by Stuart Gilbert, pp. 4-5. Used by permission.
2. William Faulkner, *Go Down, Moses* (New York: Random House, 1942), pp. 191-92. Used by permission.
3. Ibid.
4. Ibid., p. 193.
5. Ibid., p. 194.
6. Ibid., p. 204.
7. Ibid., p. 195.
8. Ibid., pp. 258-59.
9. Ibid., p. 194.

Chapter 2. Seeing

1. H. Richard Niebuhr, "Reflections on Faith, Hope and Love" (unpublished essay, mimeographed for circulation within the Yale University

Divinity School, n.d.), p. 1. Used by permission of Mrs. Florence M. Niebuhr and Richard R. Niebuhr.

2. Ibid., p. 3.
3. William F. Lynch, S.J., *Images of Hope* (Baltimore: Helicon Press, 1965), p. 243.
4. Kenneth Boulding, *The Image* (Ann Arbor, Mich.: University of Michigan Press, 1961), p. 28 (Ann Arbor Books). Used by permission.
5. Ibid., pp. 13-14.
6. Ibid., p. 174.
7. Christian *fides* or fidelity has traditionally been understood to include *fiducia*, designating trust and loyalty to the trustworthy, and *assensus*, denoting assent to truth. But it is important to recognize that *fiducia* and *assensus* represent differences of emphasis rather than different components of *fides*. Because *fiducia* tells of the relationships from which we derive our self-understanding and therefore our perspectives upon the world, it is a cognitive as well as a volitional term. Because *assensus* means conformity to the truth of Being, the end of fantasizing and the acceptance of things as they are, it includes a moral as well as a cognitive element. Because the truth that *assensus* affirms is *personal* truth, the truth of the presence of God, it is no more "intellectualistic" than is *fiducia*. Ultimately, the distinction between *fiducia* and *assensus* is simply intended to serve the claim that *fides* is an act of the whole self.
8. Stanley Hauerwas, "The Significance of Vision: Toward an Aesthetic Ethic," *Sciences Religieuses/Studies in Religion* (II, 1, pp. 36-49), pp. 37–38. I am quoting an earlier version of the essay, however, which was first circulated in mimeographed form. Used by permission of the author.

Chapter 3. Faith, Hope, and Love

1. Paul Tillich, *Love, Power, and Justice* (London: Oxford University Press, 1954), pp. 25-26. Used by permission.
2. William F. Lynch, S.J., *Images of Hope* (Baltimore: Helicon Press, 1965), pp. 90-91.
3. Jurgen Moltmann, *Theology of Hope* (New York: Harper & Row, 1967), p. 25. Used by permission.
4. Lynch, op. cit., pp. 23-24.
5. Alan Paton, *Cry, the Beloved Country* (New York: Charles Scribner's Sons, 1948), pp. 272-73. Used by permission.
6. Ibid., p. 274.
7. H. Richard Niebuhr, *Radical Monotheism and Western Culture* (New York: Harper and Brothers, 1960), p. 118. Used by permission.
8. Paul Tillich, *Dynamics of Faith* (New York: Harper and Brothers, 1957), pp. 18, 20. Used by permission.
9. Cf. David Baily Harned, *Grace and Common Life* (Charlottesville, Va.: University Press of Virginia, 1971), especially pp. 79-85. In that essay I examine the significance of the image for "choosing oneself" more extensively than I do in this context, where the primary emphasis lies upon the importance of vision. Cf. below, chapter 8, "Playing Fair."
10. Paton, op. cit., p. 277.
11. H. Richard Niebuhr, "Reflections on Faith, Hope and Love" (unpublished essay, mimeographed for circulation within the Yale University Divinity School, n.d.), p. 2. Used by permission of Mrs. Florence M. Niebuhr and Richard R. Niebuhr.

12. Moltmann, op. cit., pp. 105-6.

Chapter 4. Dialectics and Daimons

1. Jean-Paul Sartre, *Being and Nothingness* (New York: Philosophical Library, Inc., 1956), tr. by Hazel E. Barnes, p. 59. Used by permission.
2. From *Vipers' Tangle* by François Mauriac, published by Sheed & Ward, Inc., New York, pp. 241, 243. Used by permission.
3. Ibid., p. 225.
4. Ibid., p. 250.
5. Ibid., p. 29.
6. Ibid., pp. 41-42.
7. Ibid., pp. 64-65.
8. Ibid., p. 62.
9. Ibid., p. 60.
10. Ibid., p. 244.
11. From *Death of a Salesman* by Arthur Miller, p. 138. Copyright 1949 by Arthur Miller. All rights reserved. Reprinted by permission of The Viking Press, Inc.

Chapter 5. Churches

1. From *The Spire* © 1964 by William Golding, p. 92. Reprinted by permission of Harcourt Brace Jovanovich, Inc.
2. Ibid., p. 132.
3. Ibid., p. 122.
4. Ibid., p. 31.
5. Ibid., p. 103.
6. Ibid., p. 212.
7. Ibid., p. 21.
8. Ibid., p. 88.
9. Ibid., p. 136.
10. Ibid., p. 181.
11. Ibid., p. 169.
12. Ibid., p. 187.
13. Ibid., p. 160.
14. Ibid., p. 179.
15. Ibid., p. 81.
16. Ibid., pp. 202, 205-6.
17. Ibid., p. 213.
18. "Sacred Canopy" is another phrase borrowed from Peter L. Berger. See his book of that title (New York: Doubleday, 1967), especially chapters 2 and 4.
19. Ernst Wiechert, quoted by Dietrich von Oppen, *The Age of the Person* (Philadelphia: Fortress Press, 1969), p. 177. Used by permission.
20. There have been times of extraordinary social crisis when the church has believed herself called to repudiate the reigning powers entirely, but such times are rare. Christianity does not match a bias toward the stranger and alien with a bias against the establishment: there is theological necessity for the former but only contingent reasons for the latter.

Chapter 6. Strangers

1. Stanley Hauerwas, "The Christian, Society, and the Weak: A Meditation on the Care of the Retarded," *Notre Dame Magazine* Vol. 1, No. 5,

Oct. 1972. Used by permission. I am quoting an earlier unpublished version of the essay, however, with the author's permission.
2. Ibid.
3. Ibid.

Chapter 7. Temperance, Justice, and Courage

1. In Book 4 of the *Republic*, Plato examines four "cardinal" virtues, wisdom, fortitude, temperance, and justice. There, however, justice refers to the internal harmony of the self rather than to its relationships with other selves. The two most influential Christian interpretations of the cardinal virtues are Augustine, *On the Morals of the Catholic Church*, and Thomas Aquinas, *Summa Theologica*, I-II, QQ. 50-70. For useful contemporary Protestant discussions of the problems involved in a Christian interpretation of the cardinal virtues, see George F. Thomas, *Christian Ethics and Moral Philosophy* (New York: Charles Scribner's Sons, 1955), pp. 485-521, and Paul Ramsey, *Basic Christian Ethics* (New York: Charles Scribner's Sons, 1950), pp. 191-233.
2. From *The Four Cardinal Virtues* by Josef Pieper, p. 134, copyright © 1965 by Harcourt Brace Jovanovich, Inc. and reprinted by their permission.
3. Ibid., p. 201.
4. Because the virtues are concerned first of all with questions of individual conduct, this discussion of justice presupposes a relatively just social order and deals primarily with relationships between individuals. See chapter 8 for attention to the questions of the nature of a just social order and of the obligations of individuals to institutions.
5. Pieper, op. cit., pp. 52-53.
6. Ibid., pp. 111-12.
7. Noel D. O'Donoghue, ODC, "Pathos and Significance," in *Philosophical Studies* (National University of Ireland), Vol. XIX (1970), pp. 119, 124-25. Used by permission. If we do not know pathos we will never find courage, and O'Donoghue rightly concludes, "It is in fact by entering fully into the pathos of the human condition that [man] attains maturity, and has the power to give peace to others and enlarge their lives."
8. Pieper, op. cit., p. 141.

Chapter 8. Playing Fair

1. Harned, *Grace and Common Life* (University Press of Virginia, 1971), especially pp. 53-65, for arguments against the polarities, and 135-37, for an interpretation of secularization that renders them even more anomalous in the light of recent social change.
2. John Rawls, *A Theory of Justice* (Cambridge, Mass.: Harvard University Press, 1971), p. 11. © Copyright 1971 by the President and Fellows of Harvard College. Used by permission.
3. Ibid., pp. 14-15, esp.
4. Ibid., pp. 60–61.
5. Ibid., p. 250.
6. Ibid., p. 83.
7. See especially pp. 75, 100-105, ibid.
8. Ibid., pp. 101-2.
9. Ibid., p. 105.

10. Ibid., p. 75.
11. Ibid., p. 62.
12. Ibid., p. 179.
13. See especially pp. 113, 342-43, ibid.
14. Ibid., p. 112.
15. Ibid., p. 115.
16. Ibid., p. 344.
17. Ibid., pp. 114-15.
18. Ibid., p. 116. I see no particular reason why it is necessary in this context to pursue the problems that arise for defenders of "social contract" theories. I indeed prefer his mode of argument to utilitarian ways and believe that *A Theory of Justice* presents a fine account of the exigencies of playing fair within the social order.
19. Harned, op. cit., pp. 86-104. The relation between playing and creativeness is an intimate one, of course. See pp. 109-12 for a brief discussion of the way that reconciliation represents the highest form of creativity and expresses the self-transcendent capacities of the individual. Also see John B. Cobb, *The Structure of Christian Existence* (Philadelphia: Westminster Press, 1967), for an analysis of how revelation functions to transform the ways that the self understands its givenness to itself.
20. See, for example, William Poteat, "Myths, Stories, History, Eschatology and Action: Some Polanyian Meditations," in *Intellect and Hope,* ed. by Poteat and Thomas A. Langford (Durham, N.C.: Duke University Press, 1968). Also especially the splendid work of Austin Farrer in *The Glass of Vision* (Dacre Press, 1958).
21. Ian T. Ramsey, *Models and Mystery* (New York: Oxford University Press, 1964), p. 19. Used by permission of McMaster University, Hamilton, Ontario, Canada.
22. Ibid., pp. 16-17.

Chapter 9. Prudence and God

1. R. G. Collingwood, *The Principles of Art* (New York: Oxford University Press, 1938), pp. 303-4.
2. Stanley Hauerwas, "The Idea of Character." I am quoting from an unpublished paper with the author's permission. A revised version was later published in *Theological Studies,* Vol. 33, No. 4, Dec. 1972, see p. 703.
3. From *The Four Cardinal Virtues* by Josef Pieper, p. 21, copyright © 1965 by Harcourt Brace Jovanovich, Inc. and reprinted by their permission.
4. Ibid., pp. 39-40.
5. Ibid., p. 15.
6. William F. Lynch, S.J., *Images of Hope* (Baltimore: Helicon Press, 1965), pp. 177-78.

about the author

David Baily Harned is professor of religious studies at the University of Virginia, Charlottesville, where he was also department chairman from 1967 to 1972. A native of Allentown, Pennsylvania, Dr. Harned holds degrees from Yale College, Yale Divinity School, and Yale University (M.A., Ph.D.) and has also studied at New College, Edinburgh. He has been a fellow of the Society for Religion in Higher Education and of the National Endowment for the Humanities, was visiting professor of Christian studies at Punjabi University, Patiala, India, during 1970–71, and was visiting professor in the department of Christian dogmatics at the University of Edinburgh for a semester in 1972-73.

Dr. Harned's previously published books include *Theology and the Arts, The Ambiguity of Religion, Secularization and the Protestant Prospect,* and *Grace and Common Life.*